CAMPAIGN 287

TIPPECANOE 1811

The Prophet's battle

JOHN F WINKLER

ILLUSTRATED BY PETER DENNIS
Series editor Marcus Cowper

First published in Great Britain in 2015 by Osprey Publishing,
PO Box 883, Oxford, OX1 9PL, UK
PO Box 3985, New York, NY 10185-3985, USA
E-mail: info@ospreypublishing.com

© 2015 Osprey Publishing Ltd
OSPREY PUBLISHING IS PART OF BLOOMSBURY PUBLISHING PLC.

A CIP catalog record for this book is available from the British Library.

ISBN: 978 1 4728 0884 4
PDF e-book ISBN: 978 1 4728 0885 1
e-Pub ISBN: 978 1 4728 0886 8

Editorial by Ilios Publishing Ltd, Oxford, UK (www.iliospublishing.com)
Index by Alan Rutter
Typeset in Myriad Pro and Sabon
Maps by Bounford.com
3D bird's-eye views by The Black Spot
Battlescene illustrations by Peter Dennis
Originated by PDQ Media, Bungay, UK
Printed in China through Worldprint Ltd.

15 16 17 18 19   10 9 8 7 6 5 4 3 2 1

ARTIST'S NOTE

Readers may care to note that the original paintings from which the color plates in this book were prepared are available for private sale. The Publishers retain all reproduction copyright whatsoever. All enquiries should be addressed to:

Peter Dennis, Fieldhead, The Park, Mansfield, Notts, NG18 2AT, UK
Email: magie.h@ntlworld.com

The Publishers regret that they can enter into no correspondence upon this matter.

THE WOODLAND TRUST

Osprey Publishing is supporting the Woodland Trust, the UK's leading woodland conservation charity, by funding the dedication of trees.

ACKNOWLEDGMENTS

Dale Benington provided pictures from his matchless collection of early site photographs in Ohio and neighboring states, and John Stanton from his collection of photographs of early fort sites across America. James L. Graham, Robert Hart, Dan Hester, Angela Lucas, David Manges, Bobby Newsome, Catherine Wilson, Elliot Winkler, Jonathan Winkler, Sam Winkler, and Spencer Winkler took other pictures. Rick Conwell of the Tippecanoe Battlefield Museum and Lisa Ice-Jones of Grouseland provided assistance in obtaining information about the battle and surviving artifacts.

Key to military symbols

Army Group	Army	Corps	Division	Brigade	Regiment	Battalion

Company/Battery	Infantry	Artillery	Cavalry	Unit HQ	Engineer	Medical

Navy	Ordnance

Key to unit identification

Unit identifier — Parent unit
Commander
(+) with added elements
(−) less elements

CONTENTS

The Unites States in 1811

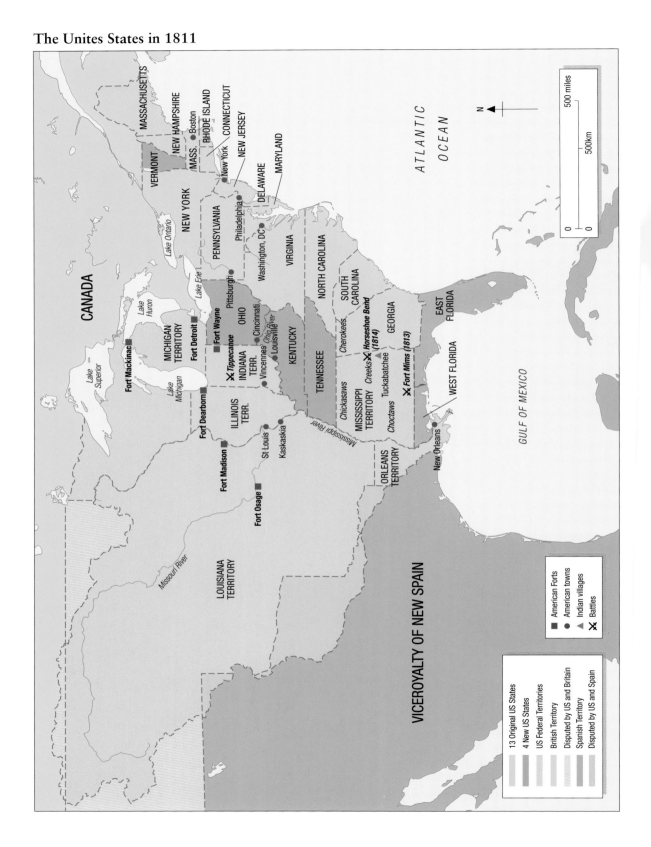

INTRODUCTION

For 40 years the Ohio Indians resisted the advance of the Americans, halting them first at the Appalachian Mountains, and then at the Ohio River. But at the August 20, 1794 battle of Fallen Timbers, Gen. Anthony Wayne's Americans defeated them. The Treaty of Greeneville followed in 1795.

For 16 years, there was peace. Hundreds of thousands of settlers emigrated to the American Northwest Frontier. But seven months before the outbreak of the War of 1812, there again was fighting. Inspired by the visions of a Shawnee shaman known as the Prophet, Indian warriors attacked an American army led by the governor of the Indiana Territory, William Henry Harrison. At the November 7, 1811 battle of Tippecanoe, Harrison, who had served at Fallen Timbers as Wayne's aide-de-camp, led the Americans to victory.

This detail from the copy of the Treaty of Greeneville in the US National Archives shows the signature of William Henry Harrison (second down on left), as a witness, and the marks of the Shawnees Black Hoof (third down on right) and Blue Jacket (bottom right). (Author's collection)

THE UNITED STATES IN 1811

In 1811, the Americans were proud of their young nation's accomplishments. It had taken them 20 years to recover from the Revolutionary War, which had left their economy and institutions in ruins. In 1788, when they had adopted the US Constitution, many had doubted that the United States would survive. But now, in the third year of the presidency of James Madison, there was prosperity and order everywhere.

Since 1788, the American population had doubled to about eight million. Then the new nation had consisted of the 13 original states, and the federal Northwest and Southwest Territories. Now it had 17 states, and six federal territories. The new states of Vermont, Kentucky, Tennessee, and Ohio, and the Indiana, Illinois, Michigan, and Mississippi Territories were on land claimed by the United States in 1788. The Louisiana and Orleans Territories were in an area of more than 800,000 square miles bought from France by the Louisiana Purchase in 1803.

Wabash River. Beyond them were the Kaskaskias, Menominees, and Winnebagos of the Illinois Territory; the Iowas, Sauks, Foxes, and Dakotas of the upper Mississippi; and the Osages west of the great river.

For centuries, the Indians had lived always in peril, ever threatened by starvation, epidemics, and raids by enemy Indian warriors. Around their villages, the women, children, and slaves worked in cornfields and vegetable patches, and gathered edible nuts and weeds. As they labored, the men came and went, hunting and warring.

Since the Treaty of Greeneville in 1795, there had been peace between the Indians and the Americans. But it had become an uneasy peace. The treaty, the Indians had believed, had defined a final border between their lands and those of the Americans. In 1803, however, there had begun to be more treaties. In the 1803 Kaskaskia Treaty and 1808 Osage Treaty, Indian tribes had asked the Americans to buy their land to create barriers to raids by their enemies the Potawatomis. But in 12 others from 1803 through 1809, the Americans had demanded more land for roads and settlements.

The Americans purchased Indian land just as they had bought Louisiana. But the Indians were not a nation like France. To evade the difficulty, the American tried to secure the agreement of every Indian tribe with any possible interest in a treaty's terms. The tribes, however, had no equivalent of the Marquis de Barbé-Marbois, who, acting as a diplomatic plenipotentiary, could bind the French to the terms of the Louisiana Purchase treaty just by signing his name. To obtain tribal assent to a treaty, the Americans tried to obtain the consent of as many important tribal leaders as possible. Some were tribal or subgroup chiefs, who held their rank by traditional rules of

Hal Sherman's *Among Gentlemen* depicts Little Turtle sitting for a portrait in Philadelphia in 1797. (Courtesy of the Hal Sherman Family)

American acquisitions of Indian Land, 1795–1809

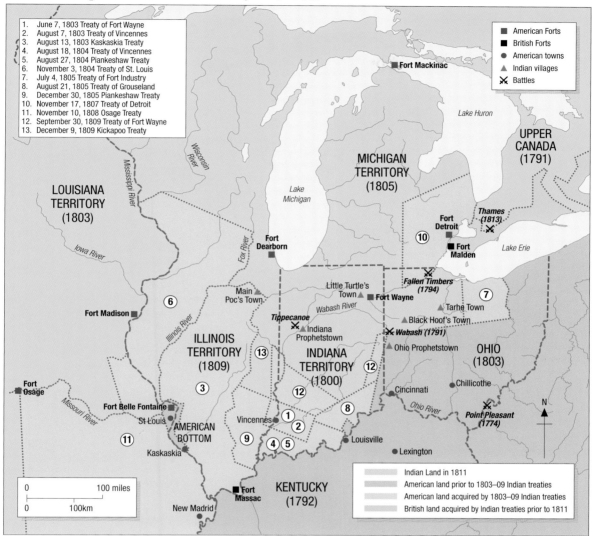

1. June 7, 1803 Treaty of Fort Wayne
2. August 7, 1803 Treaty of Vincennes
3. August 13, 1803 Kaskaskia Treaty
4. August 18, 1804 Treaty of Vincennes
5. August 27, 1804 Piankeshaw Treaty
6. November 3, 1804 Treaty of St. Louis
7. July 4, 1805 Treaty of Fort Industry
8. August 21, 1805 Treaty of Grouseland
9. December 30, 1805 Piankeshaw Treaty
10. November 17, 1807 Treaty of Detroit
11. November 10, 1808 Osage Treaty
12. September 30, 1809 Treaty of Fort Wayne
13. December 9, 1809 Kickapoo Treaty

■ American Forts
■ British Forts
● American towns
▲ Indian villages
✗ Battles

Indian Land in 1811
American land prior to 1803–09 Indian treaties
American land acquired by 1803–09 Indian treaties
British land acquired by Indian treaties prior to 1811

lineage or selection. Others were village or war chiefs. Those who agreed to the treaties could enhance their power by obtaining control of how their tribes' payments would be distributed.

The treaties, men like Madison thought, were part of a process that would end well. When settled by the Americans, an area of Indian land that produced enough food for one person might generate enough to feed 100. Where tens of thousands of Indians had subsisted, millions of Americans would prosper.

And the Indians themselves would become like the Americans. They were, the treaties recited, to use the payments they received to purchase what they needed to learn to live in a new way. In their fields, men laboring with horses and iron plows would produce crops that would end Indian hunger forever. And, in their villages, there would be Indian blacksmiths and gunsmiths, carpenters and coopers, masons and millers.

The treaties allowed the Indians to continue hunting on ceded land until it was purchased by a settler. Most of the land, moreover, was hundreds of miles beyond the nearest Americans. But the speed of settlement on the Northwest Frontier exceeded everyone's expectations. Each year, the Indians had less land upon which to hunt. And each year, their anger grew.

The Americans derived their power, thought the Shawnee shaman Penagashea, from knowledge that they should not have. The Great Spirit, the source of all good in the world, had intended the knowledge for the Shawnees. But the Americans somehow had stolen it. That injustice, he predicted, soon would be remedied. "The Great Spirit," he foresaw, "is about to restore to the Shawnees their knowledge and their rights."

Exactly how that would happen, Penagashea could not see. Some thought by war. But men like the celebrated Miami commander Little Turtle disagreed. On November 7, 1791, he had led the Ohio Indians to their greatest victory. But after they had destroyed a 1,700-man American army at the battle of Wabash, another American army had come. The Indians, counseled their greatest commander, could never overcome the Americans in a war.

An alliance of all the Indians from the Great Lakes to the Gulf of Mexico, some thought, might be able to defeat them. But men like the Shawnee war chief Blue Jacket, who had led the Indians at Fallen Timbers, thought that an idle dream. Before Point Pleasant, the Shawnee Cornstalk had vainly proposed such a league to the Senecas in the northeast and to the Cherokees, Chickasaws, Choctaws, and Creeks in the south. Before Fallen Timbers, Blue Jacket himself had traveled among the northern Indians, and his half-brother Red Pole among the southern, but their pleas had been rejected too.

Still others looked to Canada. As British allies, they thought, the Indians could defeat the Americans. But the British wanted no war with the Americans. And they too steadily bought Indian land, though in Canada they purchased it more slowly.

Peace, thought chiefs like the Shawnee Black Hoof and the Wyandot Tarhe, was the only path to better days open to the Indians. But to reach its end, they foresaw, two obstacles would have to be surmounted. Indian men, who thought any life but that of a hunter and warrior demeaning, would have to become like the men Little Turtle had seen in Philadelphia. "When I walk through the streets," he had said, "I see every person in his shop employed about something. I say to myself, which of these things can you do? Not one. I can make a bow or an arrow, catch fish, kill game, and go to war, but none of these is of any use here."

But there was reason to be hopeful. To the northeast, the Seneca shaman Handsome Lake had seen how the Indians should live in a changed world. And in the south, the Cherokees, Chickasaws, Choctaws, and Creeks already had begun to adapt successfully.

The boundaries between American and Indian land, described in treaties by reference to natural features and forts that sometimes were hundreds of miles apart, later were surveyed and marked. This walnut surveyor's stake, placed in 1797 and unearthed in 1936 in Fort Recovery, Ohio, marked the northwesternmost point of the 1795 Greeneville Treaty settlement line. (Photograph by Robert Hart)

Black Hoof lived in Black Hoof's Town, now St John's, Ohio, where this monument marks the site of his log cabin. (Photograph by Dale Benington)

The distrust of the Americans also would have to be overcome. The Indian wars had left memories that they would not forget easily. Too many mothers and fathers had been killed and scalped. Too many husbands and wives and friends had been tortured to death. Too many sons and daughters, brothers and sisters, had been carried off and never seen again.

In Ohio, however, where the settlers and Indians were in closest contact, the bitterness already had begun to fade. Horses and cattle sometimes disappeared. There were drunken fights, and even occasional murders. But the relations of the Americans and Indians were generally amicable.

The adopted Shawnee Jonathan Alder, who lived on Darby Creek in Ohio's Madison County, was optimistic. In 1782, when he had been nine, the Shawnees had killed his 16-year-old brother and taken him. But in 1805, he found his family in Virginia and convinced his surviving relatives to move to Ohio. "My mother," he remembered, "became acquainted with many of the Indians, and on the most friendly terms. I took great delight in introducing them to her. Formerly she had hated them intensely, but how wonderfully circumstances had changed things."

But the situation was unstable. In 1806, Alder recalled, "there was two or three Indians living on Darby for every white citizen… By 1811, there was but one Indian still living in Madison County." The change followed the appearance of another Shawnee shaman, who would be remembered as the Prophet.

The Indians who befriended Alder's mother included his Shawnee sister Mary and her husband, the Shawnee chief John Lewis (Quatawapea). "Never," Alder wrote, "can I express the affection I had for these two persons." This colored lithograph from McKenney and Hall's 1848 *History of the Indian Tribes of North America* reproduced an 1825 Charles Bird King portrait of Lewis, whose village is now Lewiston, Ohio. (Author's collection)

THE PROPHET AND PROPHETSTOWN

In 1805, a series of Indian villages stretched along the upper White River, in the Indiana Territory. The largest were the towns of the important Delaware chiefs Buckongahelas and Tetepachsit near present-day Muncie. One of the smallest was a Shawnee hamlet at what is now Perkinsville, Indiana. Its inhabitants included two brothers, sons of the Shawnee chief Puckeshinwa, who had fallen at Point Pleasant, and his Creek wife Methoataske. The elder, 37 in 1805, gave his name to what was called Tecumseh's Town. The younger, 30-year-old Lalawethika, had been a student of Penagashea. But since the shaman's death in 1804, he had become a drunkard, widely held in contempt.

In the spring, an illness described as a "bilious fever" swept across the Indian villages of the Northwest Frontier. When the epidemic reached the White River towns in early April, Lalawethika was found in his wigwam, apparently dead. But before he was buried, his eyes opened. He had seen, he reported, Heaven and Hell. And the Great Spirit had revealed to him that Shawnee religious practices had become so corrupt that they must be replaced. Every Shawnee dwelling must have a new fire. Every Shawnee must discard the bundle in which he kept the objects that tied him to his personal spirits.

Lalawethika then announced how the Shawnees who would reach Heaven must live. None was to drink alcohol. None was to have more than one spouse. There was to be no more stealing, fighting or raiding. Such preaching had been heard before from others. But the inspired Shawnee was an unusually powerful orator. Soon he was known by a new name, Tenskwatawa, the Open Door.

Another vision revealed to the Shawnee shaman that he and his followers were to build a new village. It was to be in Ohio, the Great Spirit had directed, on the high ground above the mouth of Mud Creek on Greenville Creek. The selection seemed ominous to some. The village, which would be known as Prophetstown, was to be on land ceded to the Americans in the Greeneville Treaty. It would, moreover, overlook Wayne's decaying Fort Greeneville, where the treaty had been signed ten years before.

The Prophet was born in 1775 in the Shawnee village of Peckuwe. This reconstruction of the village is at the site, now George Rogers Clark Memorial Park near Springfield, Ohio. (Photograph by Elliot Winkler)

12

In early 1806, a delegation of Delawares arrived at Tecumseh's Town as the Indians there were preparing to move. A month after Tenskwatawa's vision, the bilious fever had claimed the great war chief Buckongahelas. Such illnesses, some thought, should be treated by physicians, like those who had introduced inoculation against smallpox in Cincinnati in 1801. But others saw them as the work of witches, agents of the Evil Spirit who secretly spread suffering and death.

Fear of witches was widespread on the Northwest Frontier. Many Americans dreaded their power. In the new Ohio settlement of Bethel, the neighbors of Nancy Evans tried her for witchcraft in 1805. And among the Indians the worry was universal. Witches, the Delawares suspected, had killed Buckongahelas. And they asked Tenskwatawa to use his powers to find them.

He had found the witches, the Shawnee shaman announced after investigating. They were all Delawares who had adopted American customs. On March 15, 1806, the burnings began. The first to die was the Christian Delaware Ann Charity. Then it was the turn of the aged Tetepachsit. who had agreed to the Greeneville Treaty. Next came the Christian Delaware Joshua, and then Tetepachsit's nephew Billy Patterson, who shouted from the flames that he died not a witch, but "a Christian and a warrior."

On April 18, the horrified governor of the Indiana Territory sent a message to the Delawares condemning the burnings. And as to "the pretended prophet," Harrison wrote, "Ask him to cause the sun to stand still, the moon to alter its course, the rivers to cease to flow, or the dead to rise from their graves. If he does these things, you may believe that he has been sent from God."

As Tenskwatawa's followers began building Prophetstown, he toured Indian villages in Ohio to search for more witches. Among the Shawnees on the Auglaize River, he identified one, but her neighbors refused to burn her. Among the Wyandots on the Sandusky River, he found four more. They were, an early settler recalled, "the best women in the nation." But Tarhe intervened to protect them.

The rise of Prophetstown alarmed the nearest Ohioans. From the south, where settlers were building the new town of Eaton, it was only 30 miles up the road on which St Clair's and Wayne's armies had marched to their battles. From the nearest homesteads to the east, where the town of Piqua would

The most famous victim of the Prophet's witch hunts was the Wyandot Leatherlips. A signer of the Greeneville Treaty, he died on June 10, 1810. "For some imaginary evil that had been done," remembered Alder, "he was accused of witchcraft by a party of five or six Indians from Tippecanoe headed by Chief Roundhead… The whites tried hard to save the old man's life, but all to no purpose." This 1990 Ralph Helmick monument in Dublin, Ohio, honors the Wyandot chief. (Photograph by Sam Winkler)

appear in 1809, it was about the same distance on the road from Wayne's abandoned Fort Piqua.

The settlers complained to the American Indian agent at Fort Wayne, William Wells, whose brother Samuel Wells would command the Mounted Rifle Battalion at Tippecanoe. William Wells, an adopted Miami, was Little Turtle's son-in-law. But after fighting as an Indian at Wabash, he had returned to Kentucky and served as chief scout in Wayne's army.

Wells twice sent the Shawnee trader Anthony Shane with messages demanding that Prophetstown be moved to Indian land beyond the Greeneville Treaty line. The Great Spirit, the Shawnee shaman replied, had chosen the site. And his answer to Harrison's challenge, he announced, would be seen in the sky on June 16.

On a fine June Monday, crowds gathered in Indian villages across Ohio to see Tenskwatawa's response. Just before noon, the most terrifying omen known to the Shawnee began to appear. It was the *mukutaaweethee keensohtoa*, the Black Sun. "Did I not tell the truth?" Tenskwatawa shouted to a large audience at Prophetstown, before promising to restore the light.

Awed by the solar eclipse, Shawnees flocked from their villages to Prophetstown. Alder's Shawnee brother-in-law John Lewis was one of the first. Soon even Blue Jacket came from his town near Detroit.

The Great Spirit then revealed to Tenskatawa that his new religion was not just for the Shawnees. It was for all the peoples the Americans called Indians. Soon the prominent Wyandot chief Roundhead emigrated to Prophetstown from his village at what is now Roundhead, Ohio, and the Wyandot Between-the-Logs from Upper Sandusky.

Ohio governor Edward Tiffin asked the famous frontiersman Simon Kenton, who had settled in the area, to investigate. After visiting Prophetstown, he reported that the Indians there did not appear to be hostile. To reassure the settlers, Tenskwatawa dispatched Blue Jacket, John Lewis, and Tecumseh to Chillicothe, the state capital. They wanted, they told Tiffin on August 11, to live in peace with the Ohioans.

The site of Prophetstown today, as seen from across Greenville Creek in time of high water. (Photograph by David Manges)

Sitting in an amphitheater with log seats, the audiences at Prophetstown listened as Tenskwatawa revealed ever more commands by the Great Spirit. They sometimes were unexpected: "Thou shalt not suffer a dog to live," the Great Spirit had ordered.

The Indians also learned that they were to avoid as far as possible any contact with the Americans. The Great Spirit had revealed the reason, Tenskwatawa told his most trusted followers. But that was not for all to hear. The Great Spirit had created the Indians, and also the British, French, and Spanish. But the Americans, the Great Spirit had told him, "I did not make. They are not my children, but the children of the Evil Spirit."

By the spring of 1807, Tenskwatawa's fame had spread far beyond Ohio. Shamans like the Creek Seekaboo arrived from distant tribes, eager to learn the Shawnee's teachings and to carry them back to their peoples. Soon Tenskwatawa dispatched missionaries with a ritual he had devised for the initiation of converts far from Prophetstown.

The adopted Ottawa John Tanner, who had been taken at the age of ten in 1790, joined the new religion near Lake Superior in "a long lodge prepared for the solemnity." "We saw something carefully concealed under a blanket," he remembered, "in figure and dimensions bearing some relation

After the death of Little Turtle's daughter, William Wells married in 1809 Mary Geiger, the daughter of Kentucky militia Colonel Frederick Geiger, who fought at Tippecanoe. Little Turtle would die at the Fort Wayne house of William and Mary Wells on July 14, 1812. This 1810 silhouette is of Mary Geiger Wells. (Chicago Historical Museum)

Tenskwatawa's "Black Sun" was seen in Kinderhook, NY, by the Spanish astronomer José Juaquín de Ferrer. This 19th-century engraving reproduced his sketch of the total solar eclipse. (Author's collection)

to the form of a man... But while we remained, no one went near it, or raised the blanket, which was spread over its unknown contents... Four strings of beans, which we were told were made of the flesh itself of the Prophet, were carried with much solemnity to each man in the lodge, and he was expected to take hold of each string at the top, and draw them gently through his hand. This was called shaking hands with the Prophet." Despite the ceremony, Tanner remained skeptical. "I would not kill my dogs," he recalled.

Black Hoof and Tarhe reported to Wells a growing animosity between the their followers and Prophet's Indians. In May, the trouble they feared began. He had found more Shawnee witches, Tenskwatawa announced. Black Hoof and the famous Shawnee commander Black Snake were witches. Another was Captain Butler, the son of Gen. Richard Butler, who had died at Wabash, and of Cornstalk's sister, the famous female Shawnee chief Nonhelema. Indians from Prophetstown then killed two of Black Hoof's relatives.

On May 25, it grew worse. Indians visiting Prophetstown murdered the settler John Boyer near present Christiansburg, Ohio. Tiffin's successor, Thomas Kirker, dispatched messengers to the Ohio Indian villages seeking information about the killers. On June 6, Roundhead told them that Black Hoof's Shawnees had murdered Boyer. When the angry Shawnee chief learned of the accusation, he demanded a council at which its truth could be determined.

On June 24, two rival parties of 60 warriors arrived at five-year-old Springfield, a frontier settlement with 11 blockhouses and a tavern. Black Hoof and Blacksnake led one, and Roundhead and Tecumseh the other. Awaiting them was Stephen Ruddell, who would serve as a translator of the testimony to be given. After his capture and adoption as a Shawnee in 1782, Ruddell had become a boyhood friend of Tecumseh. Kenton and hundreds of Ohio militiamen also were there, waiting in a circle within which the hostile parties would meet without arms.

In 1807, Kenton lived in a cabin at this site, about 4 miles north of Springfield. (Photograph by Dale Benington)

The council almost ended before it convened. Tecumseh tried to carry with him through the circle a pipe tomahawk. Despite his furious protests that he planned only to smoke it, the militiamen confiscated the potential weapon. But the testimony failed to reveal the identities of the killers. Beyond vindicating Black Hoof, the council accomplished little.

Alarming news then reached Ohio. Two days before the council, the British frigate *Leopard* had attacked the American frigate *Chesapeake*, and seized from it four American sailors who were Royal Navy deserters. It was, cried many Americans, an act of war.

Kirker sent emissaries to the state's Indian villages, seeking pledges of loyalty in the war that seemed imminent. To Prophetstown, he dispatched Ruddell; Thomas Worthington, who had recently retired as a US Senator; and Duncan McArthur, who would win fame as a commander during the War of 1812. When they arrived on September 13, they invited Tenskwatawa to visit Chillicothe. He could not come, he said, but Blue Jacket, Roundhead, Tecumseh and a Delaware chief would.

The arrival of the four Indians in Chillicothe on September 18 caused a sensation. After camping overnight on the lawn of Adena, Worthington's new mansion, they went the next day to the Ross County courthouse, which served as Ohio's state capitol building. There they and the state's leaders met in the courtroom, where the Indians sat in the jury box and Kirker in the clerk's seat.

In words translated by Ruddell, Blue Jacket spoke for the Prophetstown Indians. They would not fight for the British, he reassured the audience. "We have deluged the country with blood to satiate our revenge," he said, "and all to no purpose. We have been the sufferers. The Great Spirit has shown us the vanity of these things. We have laid down the tomahawk, never to take it up again."

The pipe tomahawk taken from Tecumseh at the Springfield council is displayed at the Champaign County (Ohio) Historical Society Museum. (Photograph by James L. Graham)

"On Saturday morning last," reported the *Chillicothe Freedonian*, "the Governor, attended by Blue Jacket, a chief of the Shawnee nation, with three other chiefs, entered the courthouse and were engaged in talk till very late in the afternoon… Vast crowds flocked to the courthouse, led thither by the curiosity and novelty of hearing an Indian address." This reproduction of the 1801 courthouse is near its original site in Chillicothe. (Photograph by Bobby Newsome)

Adena, now a museum, as seen from the area where the Indians camped. (Author's photograph)

This colored engraving from Henry Schoolcraft's 1860 *Archives of Aboriginal Knowledge* shows Ojibwe pictographs. Drawn on a birchbark scroll, they represented the stages of a Wabeno ritual. The fourth from the bottom right shows a shaman under magical attack, with blood gushing from his mouth, and the fifth a pipe that has been poisoned. (Author's collection)

After a final reception in their honor at Adena, Blue Jacket and the others returned to Prophetstown. Tenskwatawa had remained to greet the Potawatomi chief Main Poc, who was coming from his village in what is now Kankakee River State Park in Illinois. Main Poc finally arrived with one of his six wives, displaying on his belt the many scalps he had taken in raids against the Kaskaskias and Osages. In 1806, his warriors had captured 60 Osages, killed the men, and sold the women and children to the Sauks as slaves. He was, Wells judged "the greatest warrior in the west." And even those who feared no warrior hesitated to challenge him. For the Potawatomi was a shaman too, a master in the sinister order of the Wabenos.

Usually drunk, Main Poc exemplified the conduct that Tenskwatawa had condemned after his first visions. He also had no interest in the Shawnee's new religion. He often talked to the Great Spirit himself, he told his host.

The Potawatomi chief, complained Wells, "is insufferable. He exceeds anything I ever saw." But he shared Tenskwatawa's contempt for chiefs like Little Turtle, Black Hoof, and Tarhe. And he was forming, he said, a confederacy of western Indians to fight the Americans. Prophetstown, Main Poc told the Shawnee before leaving, was in the wrong place. It should be farther west.

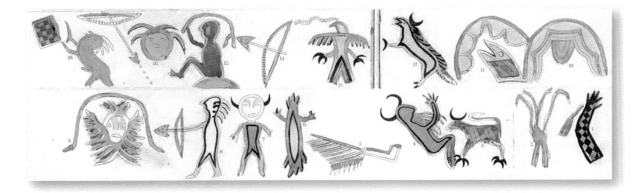

TECUMSEH AND THE NEW PROPHETSTOWN

As 1807 ended without an American declaration of war against Britain, a vision revealed to Tenskatawa that his village should be moved. The new Prophetstown was to be in the Indiana Territory, near the mouth of the Tippecanoe River on the Wabash. Blue Jacket returned to his home near Detroit, where he soon would die. Many other Indians, including a disillusioned Between-the-Logs, departed as well.

When the Prophetstown Indians went west in April, the Indiana Territory settlers already were alarmed at the prospect of Indian raids. At about the same time Boyer had been killed in Ohio, unknown Indians had attacked the Larkins family as it traveled on the Indiana Territory's main road, the Vincennes Trace. After killing her husband, they had taken Mrs Larkins and her five children as captives. Now three companies of militiamen patrolled the road.

Afraid that the conflict barely averted in Ohio now would occur in the Indiana Territory, Little Turtle led a party of Miami warriors to intercept Tenskwatawa and his followers. The Shawnee's proposed village, he told Tenskwatawa, would be on Miami land. It was not, the Shawnee replied, Miami land. It was Indian land. And on it, the Great Spirit had commanded, the new Prophetstown would rise. Unwilling to resist the emigration by force, Little Turtle and his warriors left.

As Tenskwatawa's Indians began to build their new village, a trader arrived with a British offer of food and munitions. The emissary also urged the shaman to visit Fort Malden. He would go instead, Tenskwatawa's brother responded.

With Blue Jacket gone, Tecumseh now began to emerge from his younger brother's shadow. As a young man, he had shown promise of becoming a great commander while battling Kentuckians led by Kenton at the April 9, 1792 battle of Salt Lick and April 5, 1793 battle of Reeves Crossing. He was a warrior, not a shaman. But he too had had visions.

The Americans had had their revolution, Tecumseh had seen, and now the Indians would have theirs. Like the Americans in their elections, the Indians now would choose their chiefs. Like the Americans in their states, they would continue to live in tribes, following the customs they preferred. But, like the Americans, the Indians also would become a single nation.

Tecumseh, the Great Spirit had revealed, had been born to lead the Indians through their revolution. By the time his mission reached its end, a council of chiefs would conduct the foreign relations and wars of the Indian union with other nations. And a permanent

In 1818, when Between-the-Logs (Tauyaurontoyou) succeeded Tarhe as principal chief of the Wyandots, he married Tarhe's widow, Caty Sage (Yourowquains). Between-the-Logs and Caty Sage, who at five had been kidnapped by enemies of her father and sold to Indians, then became the first Wyandot converts to Methodism. He later would become the first Wyandot Methodist minister. This engraving from Henry Howe's 1848 *Historical Collections of Ohio* preserves a sketch of the Wyandot chief by an unknown artist. (Author's collection)

boundary would divide the lands of the Indians and the Americans. Perhaps, as the leader of the new Indian union, he might be able to persuade the Americans to accept that end without war. If not, the Indians would fight. And Tecumseh would lead them.

On June 15, the Shawnee met with the aging British Indian agent Matthew Elliott and, on July 11, with Francis Gore, the Lieutenant-Governor of Upper Canada. If there was war with the Americans, Gore asked, would the Prophetstown Indians fight as British allies? If the British "should appear to be in earnest and appear in sufficient force," the Shawnee answered, the Indians would fight with them. The British, Gore said, otherwise did not want the Indians to battle the Americans. They would not, Tecumseh replied, unless the Americans took more land.

The Shawnee then began a series of travels to Indian villages that would continue for the next four years. As he spread his message of union, many Ojibwes and Ottawas migrated to the new Prophetstown. When their numbers overwhelmed the capacity of the surrounding area to feed them, Tenskwatawa asked Harrison for leave to visit Vincennes.

The Prophet arrived in July with most of the Prophetstown Indians. They were, Harrison observed "the most miserable set of starved wretches my eyes ever beheld." His enemies, Tenskwatawa told the Indiana Territory governor, had misrepresented his actions. "The religion that I have established for the last 3 years has been attended to by the different tribes of Indians," he said. "Those Indians were once different peoples. They are now but one." And they wanted, he said, peace with the Americans. A sympathetic Harrison sent to Prophetstown food, munitions, and farming tools.

Little Turtle, Tarhe, and Black Hoof had warned the Indiana Territory governor not to trust Tenskwatawa. Unless the activities at the new Prophetstown were stopped, they had said, there would be tribal civil wars. Those wars, they foresaw, would expand to include the Americans, and end in an Indian disaster. Now the powerful Potawatomi chief Winamac added his voice. Tenskwatawa, he told Harrison, was trying to persuade his warriors to forsake their tribal loyalties. He was, moreover, threatening to kill the chiefs who had agreed to the land sale treaties.

But it was Main Poc, not Tenskwatawa, whose intentions worried the Indiana Territory governor. As 1808 ended, Wells reported with delight that he had at last persuaded the Potawatomi to travel to Washington with Little Turtle to visit President Jefferson. There, as the Miami attended a series of receptions and dinners, Main Poc remained in his hotel room, leaving only on forays to find food in the surrounding woods.

At his meeting with Jefferson, the Potawatomi listened in silence as a translator repeated the American leader's words. The time of the Indian warriors, Jefferson said, was past. Now the Indians would "live in plenty and prosperity, beginning to cultivate the earth and raise domestic animals for their comfortable subsistence." But Main Poc, Little

While riding to Chillicothe to meet with Kirker, Tecumseh told Duncan McArthur that he had been born in what is now Oldtown, Ohio. This monument with a Shawnee inscription is near the site of his birth. (Photograph by Spencer Winkler)

Turtle complained to Wells, "returned as ignorant as when he went." Jefferson, the amused Potawatomi told Wells, "intended making women of the Indians."

While Little Turtle and Main Poc were in Washington, a mysterious illness appeared at Prophetstown. When surviving Ojibwes and Ottawas returned to their villages in early 1809, they reported that the illness had killed more than 150 Ojibwes and Ottawas, but only five Shawnees. Tenskwatawa, many concluded, was himself a witch, and had lured the northern Indians to his village to poison them. A party of Ottawa warriors went south to test his claim that the Great Spirit guarded Prophetstown from attack. When they returned with two Shawnee scalps, an Ojibwe and Ottawa army began to assemble. But William Hull, the governor of the Michigan Territory, stopped the action. Prophetstown, he said, was a Shawnee village under American protection.

In April, Main Poc tried to begin his war against the Americans. A Sauk and Winnebago force attempted to capture Fort Madison by deceit. But when they found the soldiers alerted and the gates closed, the Indians dispersed.

In June, Tenskwatawa tried to repeat his success in Vincennes. But Harrison, alarmed by the attempt to capture Fort Madison, had asked the trader Michael Brouillet to get information on activities at Prophetstown. The Indians there, Brouillet reported, were all eager to fight the Americans. When Tenskwatawa arrived at the Indiana Territory capital, he received a cool reception. The Prophet, Harrison wrote to the Secretary of War on July 5, was a "great scoundrel."

At the same time, Tecumseh was touring Indian villages in the west. There he used his rare oratorical powers to urge union and peace. To persuade the Indians to abandon their tribal differences and unite against a common enemy, he had to incite them to anger against the Americans. But he also had to urge restraint. The western Indians must not attack the Americans now, he warned before leaving to visit Indian villages in Ohio and New York. They must wait until all the Indians had joined his union. There must be, he pled, no more Boyers and Larkinses, and no more Fort Madisons.

Michael Brouillet lived in this 1806 house in Vincennes, now a museum. (Photograph by Angela Lucas)

The first part of his message was received everywhere with enthusiasm. The second, more difficult part, also impressed many. Although Main Poc was deaf to the Shawnee's plea for peace, the important Potawatomi chiefs Shabbona and Wabaunsee moved with their followers to Prophetstown.

When Tecumseh returned to Prophetstown, there was infuriating news. Despite his pleas, the western Indians had made another attempt to capture an American fort. In August, 140 Winnebagos had tried to capture Fort Dearborn by deceit. But, as at Fort Madison, the attempt had proved a fiasco. The other news was worse. By the September 30, 1809 Second Treaty of Fort Wayne and the December 9, 1809 Kickapoo Treaty, Delaware, Miami, Potawatomi, Kickapoo, and Wea chiefs had sold the Americans still more land.

As the snows melted in early 1810, Tecumseh set out again, this time to restore relations with the Ojibwes and Ottawas. Unwilling to attack the American forts openly, the western Indians contented themselves with raiding for horses. On May 21, Potawatomis in the Illinois Territory ambushed six Americans pursuing horse thieves, killing William Cole and three others at Cole's Ambush.

From Prophetstown, Brouillet reported to Harrison that warriors were arriving almost daily, including 30 Creeks from the south. In June, Main Poc visited briefly with a party of Potawatomis and Kickapoos. Denounced by Tenskwatawa as "an American dog," Brouillet fled to Vincennes.

After the battle of Point Pleasant in 1774, John Gibson had transcribed the famous speech of his Mingo brother-in-law John Logan. During the War of 1812, he would serve as acting governor of the Indiana Territory. This portrait by an unknown artist depicts him in 1806. (Grouseland Foundation, Vincennes, Indiana)

When warriors from Prophetstown began stealing horses and killing livestock in the Indiana Territory, Harrison sent to the village the trader Toussaint Dubois, who would lead a company of scouts at Tippecanoe. He carried a demand by Harrison that Tenskwatawa stop the actions, and an invitation for the Shawnee to visit Vincennes again.

When Tenskwatawa refused, Harrison dispatched the frontiersman Joseph Barron with another message. If the Shawnee had grievances against the Americans, it said, Harrison would arrange for him to travel to Washington. There he could ask President James Madison, who had succeeded Jefferson, to redress them.

"Brouillet was here," Tenskwatawa shouted at Barron. "He was a spy. Dubois was here. He was a spy. Now you have come." "There," he continued, pointing at the ground, "is your grave. Look upon it."

But Tecumseh, who had returned, saved Barron. He would go to Vincennes, Tenskwatawa's brother said. The invitation, the Shawnee thought, presented an opportunity. Tecumseh so far had ignored the Americans, focusing his attention instead on destroying the power of the Indian tribal chiefs. But men like Little Turtle and Winamac, who had signed the 1809 treaties, remained uncowed. To repudiate the professions of peaceful intent the Shawnee brothers previously had communicated would be a dangerous course. But if, by frightening the Americans, he could compel them to abandon the land they had purchased in 1809, the path to a rapid fulfillment of his mission would open.

On August 20, Tecumseh met Harrison and several Indian chiefs at Grouseland, the mansion of the Indiana Territory governor. Sitting in an armchair on the house's grounds, Harrison began the council with an address. Puffing on his pipe tomahawk, the Shawnee listened in silence.

"I was glad to hear your speech," Tecumseh responded when Harrison was done. "You said if we could show that the land was sold by persons that had no right to sell you would restore it. Those that did sell did not own it. It was me." And if Harrison did not rescind the treaties, he continued, "it will appear as if you wished me to kill all the chiefs that sold you the land. I tell you so because I am authorized by all the tribes to do so. I am at the head of them all… The Great Spirit has inspired me."

As the astonished Indiana Territory governor began to reply, wrote the aide recording the speeches, "Tecumseh rose up and a number of his young men with their war clubs, tomahawks and spears." First the Shawnee shouted at Winamac, who was sitting at Harrison's left. Alarmed by the words, the Potawatomi drew his pistols.

Then Tecumseh shouted at Harrison. The translator hesitated to repeat the words in English. But the adopted Delaware John Gibson, the Indiana Territory Secretary of State, needed no translator. The Shawnee, Gibson told Harrison, had called him a liar.

"Those fellows intend mischief," Gibson continued, "You had better bring up the guard." But Harrison had expected no trouble. The guard was just a sergeant and 12 soldiers from the small 7th US Infantry Regiment garrison at Fort Knox.

When Tecumseh raised his pipe tomahawk, the 75 warriors with him began to move forward. Rising from his chair, Harrison drew his sword. William Winans, a local minister, rushed onto the Grouseland portico with a musket to guard the door that led to Harrison's family. Then the moment passed. Realizing that he had gone too far, the Shawnee led his warriors away.

The sword carried by Harrison at the Grouseland council and at the battle. (Grouseland Foundation, Vincennes, Indiana)

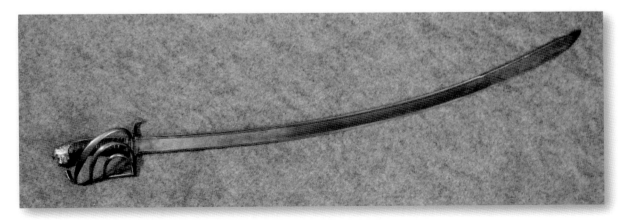

On August 21, Harrison and Tecumseh resumed their talk without further rancor. After apologizing for his outburst, the Shawnee explained the mission that he had been given by the Great Spirit. "I am alone," he told the Indiana Territory governor, "the acknowledged chief of all the Indians."

If the Shawnee brothers wanted the 1809 treaties rescinded, Harrison responded, they must go to Washington. Only President Madison could make such a decision. They would not, Tecumseh replied before leaving.

That night the Shawnee chief asked Barron to bring the Indiana Territory governor to his camp for a last meeting before the Indians left. If Madison would rescind the treaties, he told Harrison, his Indians would fight as American allies in any war against Britain. If not, he continued, they probably soon would be battling the Americans. Harrison replied with equal candor. Madison, he said, was unlikely to cancel the treaties. "It is true," Tecumseh ended the talk, "he is so far off. He will not be injured by this war. He may sit still in his town and drink his wine, whilst you and I will have to fight it out."

When reports of the confrontation at Grouseland reached Ohio, Alder remembered, "some were for leaving the country and others for forting." But the adopted Shawnee had friends at Prophetstown, who promised to warn him of any danger. "If there should be any fighting or war," they told Alder, "I should be the first to know it on Darby."

The photograph shows Grouseland, now a museum. Winans defended the door on the lower level of the mansion's portico, on the left. (Author's collection)

CHRONOLOGY

1795

August 3 — Treaty of Greeneville.

1800

May 7 — Creation of Indiana Territory. Harrison appointed Governor.

1803

February 19 — Ohio becomes the 17th state.

April 30 — Louisiana Purchase.

June 7 — First Treaty of Fort Wayne.

August 7 — First Treaty of Vincennes.

August 13 — Kaskaskia Treaty.

1804

August 18 — Second Treaty of Vincennes.

August 27 — First Piankeshaw Treaty.

November 3 — Treaty of St Louis.

1805

April — The Prophet's first vision.

June 30 — Creation of Michigan Territory.

July 4 — Treaty of Fort Industry.

August 21 — Treaty of Grouseland.

December 30 — Second Piankeshaw Treaty.

1806

April — The Prophet establishes Prophetstown in Ohio.

June 16 — The Prophet's solar eclipse.

1807

June 24 — Council in Springfield, Ohio.

September 19 — Blue Jacket, Roundhead and Tecumseh meet Ohio Governor Kirker in Chillicothe, Ohio.

November 17 — Treaty of Detroit.

1808

April — The Prophet establishes a new Prophetstown in the Indiana Territory.

July–August — Harrison's first council with the Prophet.

November 10 — Osage Treaty.

November 25 — Treaty of Brownstown.

1809

March 1 — Creation of Illinois Territory.

June 28 — Harrison's second council with the Prophet.

September 30 — Second Treaty of Fort Wayne.

December 9 — Kickapoo Treaty.

1810

August 20 — Harrison's first council with Tecumseh.

1811

June 19 — Harrison asks for federal troops.

July 27 to August 3 — Harrison's second council with Tecumseh.

Late September to early November	
	Appearance of Great Comet of 1811.
September 23–25	Harrison's army at 1st Camp.
September 26	Harrison's army reaches 2nd Camp.
September 27	Harrison's army reaches 3rd Camp.
September 28	Harrison's army reaches 4th Camp.
September 29	Harrison's army reaches 5th Camp.
September 30	Harrison's army reaches 6th Camp.
October 1	Harrison's army reaches 7th Camp.
October 2	Harrison's army reaches 8th Camp. Begins building Fort Harrison.
October 29	Harrison's army reaches 9th Camp.
October 30	Harrison's army reaches 10th Camp.
October 31	Harrison's army crosses Wabash and reaches 11th Camp.
November 1	Harrison's army reaches 12th Camp. Begins building Boyd's Blockhouse.
November 3	Harrison's army reaches 13th Camp.
November 4	Harrison's army reaches 14th Camp.
November 5	Harrison's army reaches 15th Camp.
November 6	Harrison's army reaches 16th Camp.
November 7	Battle of Tippecanoe.
November 9	Harrison's army reaches 17th Camp.
November 10	Harrison's army reaches 18th Camp.
November 19	Harrison's army back in Vincennes.
December 16	First of New Madrid Earthquakes.
1812	
June 18	US declares war on Britain.
August 16	Surrender of Detroit.
1813	
August 30	Fort Mims Massacre.
October 5	Battle of the Thames.
1814	
March 27	Battle of Horseshoe Bend.

OPPOSING COMMANDERS

AMERICAN COMMANDERS

William Henry Harrison, the governor of the Indiana Territory, led the American army. Thirty-eight in 1811, he had served at Fallen Timbers as an aide-de-camp to Anthony Wayne. During the War of 1812, he would command the American Army of the Northwest, successfully defend Ohio from British and Indian invasion, and defeat a British and Indian army at the October 5, 1813 battle of the Thames. In 1840, he would be elected the ninth president of the United States, but die of illness shortly after his inauguration. He and Vice-President John Tyler, who succeeded him, would be remembered for their campaign song, Alexander Ross's *Tippecanoe and Tyler Too.*

Harrison's staff included his college friend **Abraham Owen.** Colonel of the 18th Kentucky militia regiment, he served as an aide de camp. Owen, who had been wounded at Wabash, died at Tippecanoe.

Harrison's principal subordinates were **Col. John Parke Boyd,** who led the four-battalion Infantry Brigade; **Maj. Samuel Wells,** who commanded defense of the left flank; **Capt. Spier Spencer,** who led on the right flank; **Maj. Joseph Daviess,** who commanded the army's dragoons; and **Capt. Toussaint Dubois,** a Vincennes trader who led the army's company of scouts. Forty-seven in 1811, Boyd was commander of the US 4th Infantry Regiment. After serving from 1786 to 1788 as an ensign in the new US Army, he resigned to begin a career as a mercenary in India. After returning to the United States in 1808, he received his 4th Infantry Regiment command.

Boyd's staff included his 19-year-old aide-de-camp **George Croghan,** a nephew of George Rogers Clark and William Clark. As a US Army major, Croghan would become a national hero when he and 166 soldiers repelled an August 2, 1813 attack by 1,500 British and Indians on Fort Stephenson at present Fremont, Ohio.

Harrison was born at Berkeley Plantation, the house of his father, a signatory of the Declaration of Independence. The house is now a museum in Charles City, Virginia. (Library of Congress, Prints and Photographs Division)

Boyd's principal 4th Infantry Regiment subordinates, who were not at the battle, were **Lt. Col. Zebulon Pike and Lt. Col. James Miller.** Detached from the regiment at the time of the campaign, Pike already was a famous explorer of the Louisiana Territory. Miller, temporarily detached from the 5th US Infantry Regiment to fill Pike's position, was left to command Fort Harrison as the army advanced to Prophetstown. Three years later, he would receive a special medal from Congress for his conduct as commander of the 21st US Infantry Regiment at the July 25, 1814 battle of Lundy's Lane. In 1819, he would become the first governor of the Arkansas Territory.

At the battle, Boyd led the army's four-battalion Infantry Brigade. His principal subordinates were **Maj. George Rogers Clark Floyd** and **Capt. William C. Baen**, who led the brigade's two US Infantry battalions, and **Lt. Cols. Joseph Bartholomew** and **Luke Decker**, who commanded its two Indiana Territory militia battalions. Floyd, whose commission was in the 7th US Infantry Regiment, led the six-company Front Line US Infantry Battalion. The son and brother of Virginia governors, he had in 1810 become the commandant of Fort Knox. Baen, the senior captain of the 4th US Infantry Regiment, fell at the battle leading the three-company Rear Line US Infantry Battalion.

Floyd's senior subordinates included **Capts. Josiah Snelling** and **Zachary Taylor**. Snelling, the son of a prominent Boston banker, later would command the 5th US Infantry Regiment. Taylor, a 7th US Infantry officer who would become the 12th president of the United States, was on leave from Fort Knox at the time of the campaign. In his absence, **Lt. Jacob Albright** led his company. Among Floyd's other subordinates were **Lt. Charles Larrabee**, who led Baen's company; and **Lt. Abraham Hawkins**, who led a US Rifle Regiment company attached to the 4th Regiment for the campaign. During the War of 1812, Larrabee would lose an arm at the August 5, 1812 battle of Brownstown.

Bartholomew, the commander of the Clark County militia, was wounded leading the two-company Front Line Indiana Territory Militia Battalion.

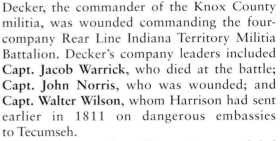

Decker, the commander of the Knox County militia, was wounded commanding the four-company Rear Line Indiana Territory Militia Battalion. Decker's company leaders included **Capt. Jacob Warrick**, who died at the battle; **Capt. John Norris**, who was wounded; and **Capt. Walter Wilson**, whom Harrison had sent earlier in 1811 on dangerous embassies to Tecumseh.

Wells, a Kentucky militia major-general, led the 4th Kentucky Militia Division. After volunteering for the campaign, he received a commission as an Indiana Territory major and command of the army's two-company Mounted Rifle Battalion. At the battle, he led the defense of the army's left flank. The leader of Kentucky companies at Wabash and Fallen Timbers, he would command the 17th US Infantry Regiment during the War of 1812. He had in 1792 persuaded his brother, the adopted Miami William Wells, to return to Kentucky. William

While commanding the 5th US Infantry Regiment, Josiah Snelling would in 1824 build Fort Snelling near St Paul, Minnesota. This stone tower from the fortress survives at the site, now Historic Fort Snelling. (Author's collection)

Wells would die at the August 12, 1812 Fort Dearborn Massacre attempting to save Samuel Wells' daughter Rebecca, the wife of the fort commandant.

Wells' company commanders were **Capts. Frederick Geiger** and **David Robb**. Geiger, a Kentucky militia colonel, led a company of volunteer Kentucky horsemen and was wounded at the battle. Two years before, his daughter Mary had married William Wells. Robb, a prominent Indiana frontiersman, led a unit of Knox County horsemen. At the battle, Wells also assumed command of a company of Indiana Territory riflemen led by **James Bigger**, a prominent Indian trader.

Spencer, who commanded on the right flank, was the sheriff of the Indiana Territory's Harrison County. He died at the battle leading a company of mounted riflemen. His subordinates included **Ens. John Tipton**. Twenty-five in 1811, Tipton, was a grandson of the famous Tennessee frontiersman Col. John Tipton. After the company's more senior officers had fallen at the battle, he assumed command. He later would be a US Senator from Indiana.

Daviess, who led the army's three-troop Dragoon Squadron, was another Kentucky volunteer. After fighting Indians at the November 6, 1792 battle of Fort St Clair, he had served as a lieutenant-colonel in the Kentucky militia. One of America's most famous lawyers, he had prosecuted Vice-President Aaron Burr at his famous 1807 trial and become the US Attorney for Kentucky. Daviess died at the battle. His subordinates were **Capts. Benjamin Parke**, **Charles Beggs** and **Peter Funk**. Parke, who led a Knox County troop, would be the first US District Court judge in Indiana. Beggs commanded a Clark County Troop. Funk, another Kentucky volunteer, was a captain in a Louisville militia dragoon squadron, from which he recruited a troop for Harrison's army.

This colored lithograph from McKenney and Hall's 1836 History of the Indian Tribes of North America reproduced an 1833 Charles Bird King portrait of Tenskwatawa. (Author's collection)

INDIAN COMMANDERS

The Indian army had an unusual commander, the Shawnee shaman **Tenskwatawa**. Called by the Americans the Prophet, he was 36 in 1811. He did not personally lead the Indian army in the engagement, but instead provided operational goals and tactical orders based upon visions that he reported to his subordinates.

The commanders at the battle led tribal units. **Mengoatowa** fell leading the Kickapoos. **Wabaunsee** commanded the Potawatomis. **Waweapakoosa** led the Winnebagos. **Roundhead** (Stiahta) commanded the Wyandots and warriors from other tribes.

OPPOSING ARMIES

AMERICAN ARMY

The American army of about 1,000 contained officers and men of two types: professional regulars and volunteer militiamen. There were approximately 325 US Army regulars. Of the 675 or so volunteer militiamen approximately 490 were from the Indiana Territory and another 85 from Kentucky. They fought in units of four types: infantrymen armed with smoothbore muskets, infantrymen armed with rifles, mounted riflemen, and dragoons.

About 605 regulars and Indiana Territory militiamen fought with muskets in the army's Infantry Brigade. The 325 regulars were in two battalions, which fought on the left of the army's two lines. The Front Line Battalion had about 205 in four 4th US Infantry Regiment companies, an attached US Rifle Regiment company armed with muskets, and a 7th US Infantry Regiment company from the garrison at Fort Knox. The Rear Battalion had about 120 in three 4th Regiment companies.

The about 280 Indiana Territory militiamen armed with muskets fought in two battalions on the right of the lines. About 80 in two companies from Knox County, which included Vincennes, were in the Front Line Battalion. The other 200, in three Knox County companies and one from Clark County, which included Charlestown, fought in the Rear Line Battalion.

All had Model 1795 US Army muskets, which could be fitted with bayonets. Designed for use in mass barrages, the weapons could be fired about three times a minute. Men with minimal training in marksmanship with the weapon could hit a target the size of a man at 50 yards.

All also carried a box with 26 paper cartridges, which contained the powder and ammunition for one firing. Instead of the usual US Army load of a ball and three buckshot, Harrison issued to his soldiers loads of 12 buckshot of about 30 caliber.

The US Springfield Model 1795 Flintlock Musket was the first musket to be mass-produced in the United States. From 1795 through 1814, about 80,000 were manufactured by a process devised by Eli Whitney. (Courtesy of NRA Museums; NRAMuseums.com; Dr William L. Roberts and Collette N. Roberts/American Liberty Firearms Collection)

The US Army soldiers wore uniforms prescribed in 1810. The 4th and 7th Regiment soldiers had high, black, visored caps decorated with a black cockade, and white cord, tassel, and plume. They wore blue coatees closed across the chest with hooks and eyes, white pantaloons (black overalls in winter), and black gaiters and shoes. The Rifle Regiment men had bearskin-crested caps and green coatees, pantaloons, and gaiters.

Those assigned to sentry duty were given heavy wool "watchcoats." Other soldiers were issued extra flannel shirts and mittens. Many also purchased with their own funds "blanket coats," belted heavy wool blankets cut to expose heads and sleeve arms.

The regular officers wore long, lapeled blue coats, closed across the chest with hooks and eyes; a white belt across the chest holding a scabbard; white pantaloons; and black boots. Most had abandoned tricorn hats for the bicorn *chapeau bras*, which had a cockade and white plume. In bad weather, they usually wore woolen cloaks.

The militiamen dressed in the usual clothes of western settlers. They wore wide-brimmed black hats, western fringed hunting shirts or collarless shirts, "Kentucky jeans" made of buckskin or linen, and shoes or moccasins. Some wore their hunting shirts over collarless shirts as light jackets known as "hunting frocks."

Twenty-year-old John Mills, the musician of Capt. Josiah Snelling's company, remained in the US Army for another 50 years. In this May 1861 retirement photograph, he is wearing the uniform of a US Army sergeant. (Library of Congress, Prints and Photographs Division)

Militia company captains often had their men wear hunting shirts or frocks of the same color, sometimes with fringe in a contrasting color. The dress of some officers resembled that of US Army officers. Others were indistinguishable from their men.

Of the about 250 militiamen who fought as riflemen, 190 were from the Indiana Territory and the rest from Kentucky. Those on horseback were in the army's two-company Mounted Rifle Battalion, which included a 60-man Knox County company and a 60-man company of Kentucky volunteers; and in a detached 85-man Harrison County company. Those on foot were in a 45-man Clark County company.

The riflemen carried their personal weapons, the about 52-caliber Kentucky long rifles of western frontiersmen. Minimally competent riflemen could hit with a lead ball a target the size of a man's head at 100 yards. The weapons, however, took twice as long to load as muskets.

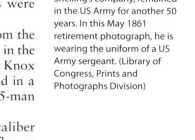

The weapons also lacked bayonets. For close combat, the riflemen instead used tomahawks, and knives with long blades. "The large knife and hatchet which constituted a part of their equipment," remembered Adam Walker, the musician in Lt. Abraham Hawkins' US Rifle Regiment company, "with their dress, gave them rather a savage appearance." The riflemen's dress was identical to that of the musket-bearing militiamen.

About 130 men fought in the army's three-troop Dragoon Squadron, which included a 75-man Knox County troop, a 30-man Clark County Troop, and a troop of 25 Kentucky volunteers. The weapons and uniforms of Parke's and Beggs' men probably were similar to those of Funk's. Each of the Kentuckians, Maj. Joseph Daviess directed, was to carry a pistol and "12 cartridges… to consist of such a number of buck-shot as the caliber of the pistol will permit." Their dress, he ordered, was to be "a blue coatee with pantaloons, without any scarlet, a hat or cap covered with bearskin, boots and spurs."

Harrison's soldiers varied widely in age and experience. Spier Spencer's 12-year-old son George fought in his father's company. Isaac White, colonel of the Illinois Territory militia regiment, died at the battle serving as a private in Parke's dragoon troop.

Because the last fighting with Indians had been 16 years before, many of the officers and most of the men had no combat experience. In the short time available, Harrison followed as much as possible the training model used by Wayne during his Fallen Timbers campaign, which included mock battles with men dressed as Indians and using Indian weapons and tactics.

Despite their lack of experience and training, the Americans fought at Tippecanoe with high morale. During his brief tenure as their commander, Harrison won the enthusiastic loyalty of both his US Army and militia soldiers. "The confidence of the troops in the general," recalled Adam Walker of Hawkins' 4th Regiment company, "was unlimited." His treatment of his men, Walker said, "fixed in the breast of every soldier an affectionate and lasting regard for their general, the benefit of which was fully realized in the conduct of the troops in the engagement, as well as throughout the campaign."

INDIAN ARMY

This war club, carried by a warrior at Tippecanoe, was found on the battlefield by one of Harrison's aides. (Grouseland Foundation, Vincennes, Indiana)

The about 500 warriors in the Indian army fought in tribal groups. Most were in 125-warrior units of Kickapoos, Potawatomis, and Winnebagos. Another 125 Shawnees, Wyandots, and Indians from other tribes fought in smaller contingents. All but the Winnebagos spoke either Iroquoian or Algonquian languages. Most could communicate with one another in varying degrees of fluency. The Winnebago language, however, was from a different linguistic family, Siouan. Communication with them often required interpreters. The Indians, Harrison would write to Kentucky Governor Charles Scott after the battle, "were much better armed than the greater part of my troops." They generally preferred smoothbore to rifled firearms. Most probably had .75-caliber British Land Pattern and

.69-caliber Charleville muskets, from which they fired rounds of one large ball, and three smaller balls of as little as .25 caliber. For close combat, they carried tomahawks or war clubs, and also knives. The Indians, moreover, had learned from Wayne's devastating bayonet charge at Fallen Timbers. Most, Harrison observed, carried spears.

By 1811, the apparent ease with which Wayne had defeated the Indians at Fallen Timbers had caused many Americans to forget their spectacular success at Wabash. Men like Lt. Adam Larrabee of the US Light Artillery Regiment assumed that the Indians were incapable of defeating a large force of US Army regulars. When he learned that his cousin, 4th US Infantry Regiment Lt. Charles Larrabee, had been dispatched to join Harrison's army, he wrote to console his cousin on his assignment to fight such enemies rather than British or French soldiers.

"You speak light of battles with Indians," his cousin testily replied. "I say that an American army deserves more credit in fighting Indians than any army in the world... In fighting an English or French army or where some mercy is shown on both sides as respects prisoners, there is some hope remaining if beaten, but with Indians none has ever been granted... The army were correctly informed before they left Fort Harrison that the Prophet was determined to burn alive all prisoners."

By 1811, many Indians opposed such brutality. "I frequently," Alder remembered, "heard the Indians argue against it, and the main reason was that when the whites took prisoners, they invariably treated them well." But painted to present a terrifying appearance, the Indians also brought with them to Tippecanoe a reputation for cruelty that intimidated their enemies.

The Indians' psychological advantage over his soldiers was of less concern to Charles Larrabee's commander than their prowess in combat. Trained from boyhood in the skills needed for warfare in the western woods, the Indians would fight with friends, all eager to prove their courage. Led by superb commanders at the right of each of their small units of 10 to 20 warriors, they would try to execute deftly tactical maneuvers that had been perfected in centuries of battles with other Indians.

The Indians, Harrison knew, had little doubt that they could defeat a much larger American army. And their confidence, he thought, was not unfounded. The men his soldiers would face, the American commander judged, were "the finest light infantry troops in the world."

ORDERS OF BATTLE

TIPPECANOE, NOVEMBER 7, 1811

Killed or mortally wounded (K)
Wounded (W)
Commander Not Present (NP)
Detached for other service (D)

AMERICAN (1,000)[1]

Governor William Henry Harrison, Commander
Col. Abraham Owen, Aide-de-camp (K)
COMPANY OF SCOUTS OF CAPT. TOUSSAINT DUBOIS (15)

INFANTRY BRIGADE (four battalions) (605)

Col. John Boyd, Commander
George Croghan, Aide-de-camp
FRONT-LINE US INFANTRY BATTALION (six cos.) (205)
Maj. George R. C. Floyd, Commander
Company of Capt. William C. Baen (D) (K) (40)
Lt. Charles Larrabee, Acting Commander
Company of Capt. Josiah Snelling (40)
Company of Capt. George W. Prescott (40)
Company of Capt. Return B. Brown (35)

US Rifle Regiment Company of Lt. Abraham Hawkins (30)[2]

7th US Infantry Regiment Company of Lt. Jacob Albright (20)[3]

FRONT-LINE INDIANA TERRITORY MILITIA BATTALION (two cos.) (80)

Lt. Col. Joseph Bartholomew, Commander (W)

Company of Capt. Thomas Scott (40)

Company of Capt. Andrew Wilkins (40)

REAR-LINE US INFANTRY BATTALION (three cos.) (120)

Capt. William C. Baen, Commander (K)

4th US Infantry Units

Company of Capt. Robert C. Barton (40)[4]

Company of Capt. Joel Cook (40)

Company of Lt. George Peters (40)[5]

REAR-LINE INDIANA TERRITORY MILITIA BATTALION (four cos.) (205)

Lt. Col. Luke Decker, Commander (W)

Company of Capt. Walter Wilson (40)

Company of Capt. William Hargrove (55)

Company of Capt. Jacob Warrick (K) (55)

Company of Capt. John Norris (W) (50)

LEFT FLANK (three cos.) (165)

Maj. Samuel Wells, Commander

Mounted Rifle Company of Capt. Frederick Geiger (W) (60)

Mounted Rifle Company of Capt. David Robb (60)

Rifle Company of Capt. James Bigger (45)

RIGHT FLANK (one co.) (85)

Capt. Spier Spencer, Commander (K)

Mounted Rifle Company of Capt. Spier Spencer (K) (85)[6]

DRAGOON SQUADRON (three troops) (130)

Maj. Joseph H. Daviess (K), Commander

Dragoon Troop of Capt. Benjamin Parke (75)

Dragoon Troop of Capt. Charles Beggs (30)

Dragoon Troop of Capt. Peter Funk (25)

INDIAN (500)[7]

The Prophet (Tenskwatawa), Commander

Potawatomi (125)

Wabaunsee, Commander

Kickapoo (125)

Mengoatowa, Commander (K)

Winnebago (125)

Waweapakoosa, Commander

Other Tribes (125)

Roundhead, Commander

1. Estimates of the number of Americans at the battle have ranged from 800 to more than 1,200. The numbers given are based upon Tipton's statement that, on October 29, the army consisted of "about 640 foot and 270 mounted;" Harrison's later estimate was that there were 250 regulars at the battle, and rosters of individual units.

2. Also known as the company of Capt. Moses Whitney, who had resigned in July 1811.

3. Also known as the company of its former commander, Capt. Thornton Posey, who had fled from Fort Knox on June 24, 1811, after killing Lt. Jesse Jennings; and of its current commander, Capt. Zachary Taylor, who was in Maryland at the time of the campaign.

4. A small unit known as "Welch's Company," led by Lt. Oliver Burton, was incorporated into this company during the campaign.

5. Also known as the company of its former commander, Capt. Paul Wentworth, and of its commander, Lt. Charles Fuller, who led the company until October 29, and later would resume command.

6. Smaller companies led by Capts. Thomas Berry and Zachariah Lindley were incorporated into this unit.

7. Estimates of the number of Indians at the battle have ranged from 350 to 1,000.

OPPOSING PLANS

AMERICAN PLAN

Harrison's campaign had two goals. Its primary objective was to disperse the Indians concentrated at Prophetstown. While they remained, Vincennes was vulnerable to a surprise attack against which the Indiana Territory capital could not be continuously protected.

The campaign's second objective was to disrupt the attempts of Tecumseh to persuade warriors from many tribes to unite in a war against the Americans. The Shawnee's temporary absence from Prophetstown, Harrison believed, provided an opportunity for a battle in which the Americans could defeat and demoralize the Indians. Those at Prophetstown, he expected, would either attack his advancing army or, by refusing to abandon their village, justify such a battle.

In planning his campaign, Harrison drew on his experience as an aide-de-camp to Anthony Wayne during Wayne's 1793 and 1794 campaigns in Ohio. In every aspect of his effort, he applied what he had learned during his service with the great commander.

The first was the great danger that his men would starve. Like Wayne's soldiers, his would eat each day a half-pound of beef, provided by a herd of cattle that would accompany the army. They also would consume daily the bread made from 18 ounces of flour that must be transported by packhorses, wagons that required the construction of roads, or watercraft.

Tecumseh carried with him on his travels this chest, which is displayed at Fort Malden National Historical Site in Amherstburg, Ontario. (Courtesy of Parks Canada Agency)

The geography and terrain of Harrison's area of operations diminished the logistical problems that Wayne had barely surmounted. The Wabash River allowed water transport to Prophetstown. Much of the surrounding area, moreover, was flat grassland over which roads could easily be cut.

Harrison decided for the first part of his advance to use the Wabash for transport, and then to follow a prairie route to Prophetstown. By such a route, he believed, his men could advance quickly with a barely adequate food supply. They also might be able to reach Tenskwatawa's village undetected by enemy scouts.

Western Ohio and the Indiana Territory in 1811

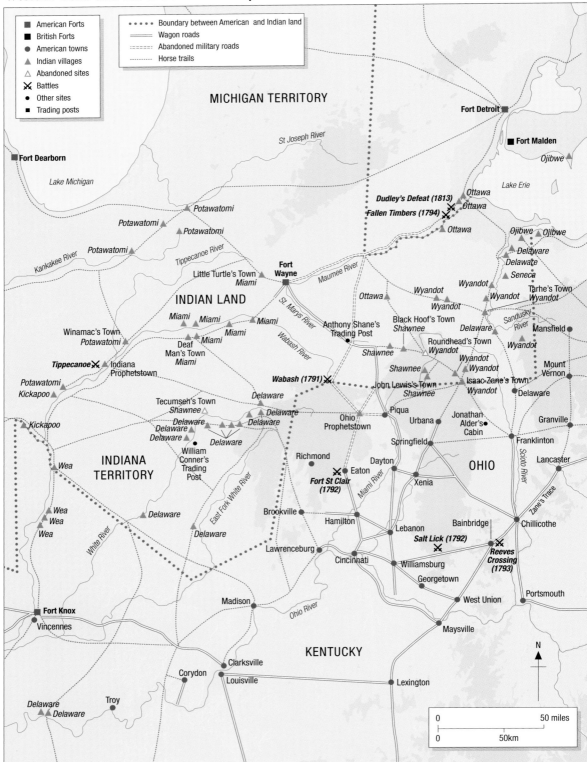

Legend:
- ■ American Forts
- ■ British Forts
- ● American towns
- ▲ Indian villages
- △ Abandoned sites
- ✕ Battles
- ● Other sites
- ■ Trading posts

- ••••• Boundary between American and Indian land
- ══ Wagon roads
- ═══ Abandoned military roads
- ⋯⋯ Horse trails

MICHIGAN TERRITORY

St Joseph River

Fort Detroit

Fort Malden

Ojibwe

Fort Dearborn

Lake Michigan

Lake Erie

Potawatomi

Potawatomi

Potawatomi

Kankakee River

Tippecanoe River

Potawatomi

Ottawa

Ottawa

Dudley's Defeat (1813)

Fallen Timbers (1794)

Ottawa

Little Turtle's Town
Miami

Fort Wayne

Maumee River

Ojibwe   Ojibwe

Delaware

Delaware

Seneca

INDIAN LAND

St Marys River

Ottawa

Wyandot

Wyandot

Tarhe's Town
Wyandot

Miami   *Miami*

Miami

Miami

Wabash River

Anthony Shane's
Trading Post

Black Hoof's Town
Shawnee

Wyandot

Delaware

Wyandot

Mansfield

Winamac's Town
Potawatomi

Deaf
Man's Town
Miami

Miami

Shawnee

Roundhead's Town
Wyandot

Wyandot

Sandusky
River

Wyandot

Mount
Vernon

Tippecanoe ✕

Potawatomi
Kickapoo

Indiana
Prophetstown

Tecumseh's Town
Shawnee △

Delaware

Shawnee

Wabash (1791) ✕

John Lewis's Town
Shawnee

Wyandot

Isaac Zane's Town
Wyandot

Delaware

Granville

Kickapoo

Delaware

Delaware

Delaware
Delaware

Delaware

Ohio
Prophetstown

Piqua

Urbana

Jonathan
Alder's
Cabin

**INDIANA
TERRITORY**

Wea

William
Conner's
Trading
Post

East Fork White River

Springfield

Richmond

Dayton

OHIO

Franklinton

Lancaster

Eaton

Xenia

Wea
Wea

Delaware

Delaware

**Fort St Clair
(1792)** ✕

Zane's Trace

Wea

White River

Brookville

Hamilton

Lebanon

Bainbridge

Chillicothe

Lawrenceburg

Cincinnati

Williamsburg

Salt Lick (1792) ✕

**Reeves
Crossing
(1793)** ✕

Madison

Georgetown

West Union

Portsmouth

Ohio River

Maysville

Fort Knox
Vincennes

KENTUCKY

N

Corydon

Clarksville

Louisville

Lexington

Delaware
Delaware

Troy

0	50 miles
0	50km

The Michigan Territory and Northern Illinois Territory in 1811

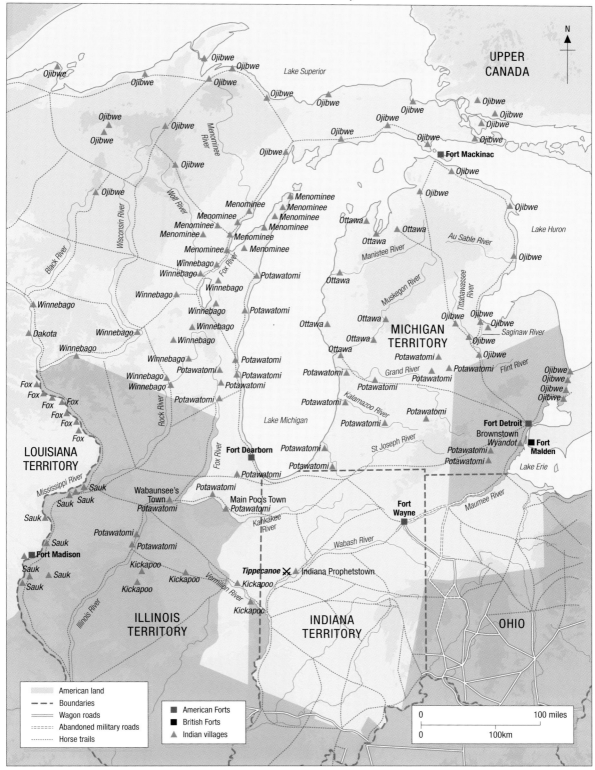

N

UPPER CANADA

Lake Superior

Ojibwe
Ojibwe
Ojibwe
Ojibwe
Ojibwe
Ojibwe
Ojibwe
Ojibwe
Ojibwe
Ojibwe
Ojibwe
Ojibwe
Ojibwe
Ojibwe
Ojibwe
Ojibwe
Ojibwe
Ojibwe
Ojibwe
Ojibwe
Ojibwe
Ojibwe
Ojibwe
Ojibwe
Ojibwe

■ Fort Mackinac

Menominee River
Wolf River
Menominee
Menominee
Menominee
Menominee
Menominee
Menominee
Menominee
Menominee
Menominee
Menominee
Menominee
Menominee

Ottawa
Ottawa
Ottawa
Ottawa
Ottawa
Ottawa
Ottawa
Ottawa

Lake Huron
Au Sable River
Manistee River
Muskegon River

MICHIGAN TERRITORY

Tittabawassee River
Saginaw River
Flint River

Ojibwe
Ojibwe
Ojibwe
Ojibwe
Ojibwe
Ojibwe
Ojibwe

Winnebago
Winnebago
Winnebago
Winnebago
Winnebago
Winnebago
Winnebago
Winnebago
Winnebago
Winnebago
Winnebago
Winnebago
Winnebago
Winnebago

Wisconsin River
Black River

Dakota

Fox River

Potawatomi
Potawatomi
Potawatomi
Potawatomi
Potawatomi
Potawatomi
Potawatomi
Potawatomi
Potawatomi
Potawatomi
Potawatomi
Potawatomi
Potawatomi
Potawatomi
Potawatomi
Potawatomi
Potawatomi
Potawatomi
Potawatomi
Potawatomi

Grand River
Kalamazoo River
Lake Michigan
St Joseph River

Rock River

Fox
Fox
Fox
Fox
Fox
Fox
Fox

LOUISIANA TERRITORY

Mississippi River

Sauk
Sauk
Sauk
Sauk
Sauk
Sauk
Sauk
Sauk
Sauk

■ Fort Madison

■ Fort Dearborn

Wabaunsee's Town
Potawatomi

Main Poc's Town
Potawatomi

Kankakee River

Potawatomi
Potawatomi
Potawatomi

Kickapoo
Kickapoo
Kickapoo
Kickapoo
Kickapoo

Vermilion River
Illinois River

ILLINOIS TERRITORY

Ojibwe
Ojibwe
Ojibwe
Ojibwe

■ Fort Detroit
Brownstown
Wyandot
■ Fort Malden
Lake Erie

Tippecanoe ✕ Indiana Prophetstown

■ Fort Wayne

Maumee River
Wabash River

INDIANA TERRITORY

OHIO

Legend

▨ American land
- - - Boundaries
═══ Wagon roads
┅┅┅ Abandoned military roads
········ Horse trails

■ American Forts
■ British Forts
▲ Indian villages

| 0 | 100 miles |
| 0 | 100km |

37

In 1794, Wayne had deceived Indian scouts about the objective toward which he was marching by cutting a road in one direction and advancing in another. Harrison would create a similar deception. After advancing on a road cut along an Indian trail up the east bank of the Wabash, he would have the road built for several miles ahead. Then his army would quickly leave it, cross the Wabash and advance through the prairie beyond the river's west bank.

Harrison also had learned from Wayne how to respond to an Indian attack while his army marched or was encamped. Indian tactics, he knew, were intended to minimize casualties and relied upon the force protection that the western woods provided. Attacking Indians would attempt to surround his army. Then, by small unit maneuvers, they would try to inflict so many casualties that the Americans would break through the encirclement and flee. But at Fallen Timbers, he had seen Wayne defeat such tactics by careful deployment of his marching units, and skillful redeployment after attack. As if by magic, units appearing in the right locations had stopped the Indians from encircling Wayne's army, forced them to fight in an opposing line, and driven them from the field in a rout.

When Harrison arrived at Prophetstown on November 6, the Indians asked him to encamp and attend a council on November 7. The next day, Harrison believed, the Indians would refuse to disperse. His army then would attack Prophetstown, which was fortified with elaborate log breastworks. American casualties in such an attack, he concluded, would be reduced if the assault was made in darkness. "It was my determination," he later wrote, "to attack and burn the town the following night."

The only American commander to have fought Indians in a significant night battle had been Wayne, whose soldiers' bayonets had driven 300 Creeks from his camp near Savannah in the June 24, 1782 battle of Ebenezer Creek.

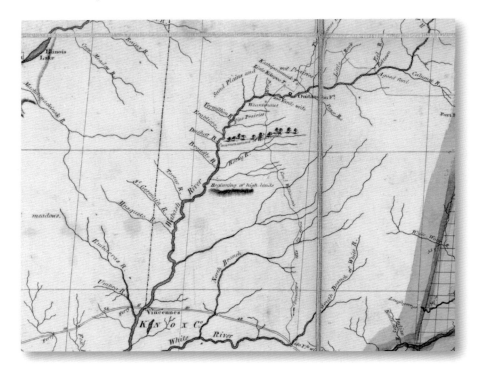

This detail from Abraham Bradley's 1804 *Map of the United States* shows Harrison's area of operations. (Library of Congress, Geography and Map Division)

In such a battle, Harrison knew, darkness made it difficult for the Indians to execute their usual tactics. The ratio of Indian to American casualties in a night battle, he estimated, would be three times as high as that in a battle in daylight.

Because of the disadvantages they would face, Harrison thought it unlikely that the Indians would attack his encamped army during the night before the council. If they did, he believed, an American victory would depend upon the extent to which his soldiers could retain their order. "In night attacks," Harrison would write, "discipline always prevails over disorder. The party which is able to preserve its order longest must succeed." It also would depend upon the facility with which American units could redeploy to areas where the Indians threatened to break through the camp perimeter. "Perhaps," Harrison would write after Tippecanoe, "there never was an action where (for the number of men engaged) there were so many changes of position performed."

INDIAN PLAN

When the Americans advanced toward Prophetstown, the Indians were eager to attack. Tecumseh, however, had ordered them to avoid any battle in his absence. "Had I been at home," he later said, "there would have been no blood shed at that time."

When the Americans appeared at Prophetstown, the Indians sought from Tenskwatawa guidance on how to respond. For centuries, information provided by Indian shamans had shaped the tactical decisions of Indian commanders. On October 22, 1790, for example, such intelligence had forced Little Turtle to abandon a planned attack on an American army led by Brigadier-general Josiah Harmar. Ottawa shamans had interpreted a lunar eclipse as an omen of high casualties in such an engagement.

When the Americans arrived at Prophetstown, a vision revealed to Tenskwatawa that, if Harrison were killed, the Americans would be left unable to defend themselves from an Indian attack. He recommended an assassination at the November 7 council. When the impatient Indians demanded immediate action, he saw in another vision that Harrison could be killed that night.

The Indian commanders then quickly designed a night operation. As assassins infiltrated the American camp, an advancing crescent of Indians would encircle the American camp in silence. When the infiltrators signaled that they had killed Harrison, the Indians would attack the camp's helpless defenders.

"I am determined," Harrison wrote to Kentucky Governor Charles Scott, "to disperse the Prophet's banditti before I return or give him the chance of acquiring as much fame as a warrior as he has as a saint." This early 19th-century wood engraving by the French architect, artist, and antiquary Jean-Nicholas Huyot depicts the Prophet awakening after a vision. (Library of Congress, Prints and Photographs Division)

CAMPAIGN AND BATTLE

THE BEGINNING OF HARRISON'S CAMPAIGN

Two weeks after Tecumseh's dramatic meeting with Harrison at Grouseland, Indian chiefs began arriving for a council in Brownstown, the Michigan Territory village of the adopted Wyandot Adam Brown. Infuriated by Tecumseh's claim to be "alone the acknowledged chief of all the Indians," they condemned the actions of the Shawnee brothers. Chiefs at a Fort Wayne council in October made a similar declaration.

The actions of the chiefs seemed to reveal that Tecumseh's grand claims at Grouseland had been empty boasts. But Harrison was unsure. At the Fort Wayne council, the important Miami chief Pacanne, who had signed the 1809 Fort Wayne Treaty, announced that he now opposed it. The land that had been sold, he said, must never be settled. And from trusted sources Harrison heard reports that chiefs were being shunned or replaced by warriors loyal to Tecumseh.

As the chiefs had met at Brownstown and Fort Wayne, Tecumseh had been visiting villages of the Iowas, Sauks, Foxes, and Menominees. Then he had gone again to Fort Malden. If there was war between the British and Americans, he told Elliott on November 15, his Indians would fight with the British. In return, he wanted the British to provide munitions and supplies for any war the Indians waged against the Americans.

"Before next autumn and before I visit you again," Tecumseh told Elliott, "the business will be done." The alarmed British Indian agent asked the Shawnee what he meant by "the business." The British, Elliott insisted, wanted no Indian war against the Americans. He meant, Tecumseh responded, only the completion of his Indian confederacy.

The appearance today of the site of Fort Malden, now Fort Malden National Historic Site in Amherstburg, Ontario. (Photograph by John Stanton)

There would be no war yet. In 1811, he would travel three more times. First, after making a last appeal at Ohio villages, he would travel to Ottawa and Ojibwe towns in the far north. Next he would go south, to the Chickasaws, Choctaws, and Cherokees; and to his mother's people, the Creeks. And then he would visit the Osages in the west.

It was in 1812 that the war would come. Only by such a war, the Shawnee now saw, could his Indian revolution be realized. The carnage would be horrific. And men like Main Poc, he knew, would glory in it. As it raged from the Great Lakes to the Gulf of Mexico, Americans would flee in tens of thousands across the Appalachian Mountains. And then would come peace, and the completion of his mission.

Unlike his brother, Tecumseh had American friends. He often visited the family of James Galloway in this 1798 cabin near his birthplace. (Courtesy of the Greene County (Ohio) Historical Society. Photograph by Catherine Wilson)

In May 1811, William Wells learned that two of the Potawatomis who had killed Cole and the other Illinois Territory men were at Prophetstown. He and the Delaware trader John Conner then traveled to Tenskwatawa's village to demand their surrender. There he talked with Tecumseh, who was about to depart on the first of the year's journeys. After refusing to surrender the Potawatomis, the Shawnee said that he would stop any further American settlement. He would never succeed, the Indian agent responded. Wells, Tecumseh replied, "would live to see the contrary."

As Wells and Conner returned to Fort Wayne without the Potawatomis, fear of war spread across the frontier. In the Louisiana Territory, an Iowa visiting St Louis in May was overheard saying to another, "The time is drawing near when the murder is to begin, and all the Indians that will not join are to die with the whites." In the Illinois Territory, Potawatomis killed a man and carried off his sister. In the Indiana Territory, Weas forced surveyors who entered the land ceded in the 1809 treaties to flee. Settlers reported that horses had been stolen and cattle slaughtered. Expecting worse, those on the East Fork of the White River posted a permanent militia garrison at a new stronghold, Fort Vallonia.

This 1805 structure in Vincennes, now a museum, served as the Indiana territorial capitol building. (Photograph by Angela Lucas)

Despite the unrest, Harrison dispatched up the Wabash boats carrying the annual salt payment due the Indians under the 1803 Fort Wayne Treaty. On June 18, the frightened boatmen returned early. The Indians at Prophetstown, they reported to Harrison, had seized the salt.

And there, they said, they'd seen a fleet of canoes large enough to carry 800 warriors. A startled Harrison then had his own vision. Moving by water, he realized, an Indian army could attack Vincennes faster than any warning could reach him. In time of high water, he calculated, it could reach the Indiana Territory capital in as little as 24 hours.

The Indiana Territory governor took immediate action to diminish the capacity of the Indians to attack. Warriors regularly brought muskets needing repair to the Vincennes shop of Thomas Jones and his adopted Indian son, Piankeshaw Dick. When 15 Indians arrived with a new load of broken firearms, Harrison banned any further repair work.

Harrison also asked for help. There were 600 warriors at Prophetstown, he wrote on June 19 to US Secretary of War William Eustis, "and Tecumseh is daily expected with a considerable reinforcement from the lakes. I have not the least doubt that a crisis with this fellow is approaching. His determination is to come to this place with as many men as he can raise and, if the land which was lately purchased is not immediately given up, to commence the war." "Permit me," he continued, "to recommend that the troops that are now at Pittsburgh be ordered here immediately."

The Indiana Territory governor then asked Joseph Barron to take Capt. Walter Wilson, who would lead a militia company at Tippecanoe, to Prophetstown with a letter to Tecumseh. It was a dangerous mission. And the opening words of the letter reflected Harrison's fears. "My friend Tecumseh," it began, "the bearer is a good man and a brave warrior. I hope you will treat him well. You are yourself a warrior, and all such should have esteem for each other."

On July 3, Barron and Wilson reached the Indian town, where Tecumseh had returned from his first trip. The Potawatomis who had killed Cole and the others must be surrendered, the letter told him. And neither he nor Tenskwatawa was to approach Vincennes with a large party of warriors.

Tecumseh's prior visit to the Indiana Territory capital had failed to persuade the Americans to rescind the 1809 treaties. But the Shawnee's dramatic defiance had frightened the Indian chiefs. Harrison did not know that many now had secretly recognized Tecumseh's authority. Many others, however, still opposed him. That some were with Harrison in Vincennes presented an opportunity to deliver before traveling south a stroke that would end further resistance.

On July 4, Barron and Wilson left Prophetstown with Tecumseh's reply. "I will be with you myself in eighteen days," the Shawnee had said. "When I come to Vincennes and see you, all will be settled in peace and happiness."

BELOW
After fighting with Tecumseh during the War of 1812, Shabbona would become a leading advocate of peace with the Americans. This photogravure from a 1908 edition of John Wakefield's *History of the Black Hawk War* reproduced a photograph of Shabbona in 1859, when the Potawatomi was 84. (Author's collection)

Tecumseh had promised, Wilson reported to Harrison, not to bring with him a large party of warriors. But the Indiana Territory governor feared another surprise. After sending his family to safety in Kentucky, he dispatched scouts up the Wabash.

Soon word arrived at Grouseland that 53 canoes were descending the river, carrying about 300 warriors and 30 women and children. On July 25, Wilson intercepted the Indian fleet at the mouth of Busseron Creek. Why, he asked Tecumseh, had the Shawnee broken his promise? Only 24 warriors were with him, Tecumseh replied. The other Indians had just decided to visit Vincennes.

By July 27, when Tecumseh arrived at the Indiana Territory capital, Harrison's scouts had discovered that Indian warriors were concealed in the woods all around the town. But this time the Shawnee found waiting in Vincennes a guard of more than a sergeant and 12 men. He met, a witness remembered, "bayonets fixed and glistening in every direction." Harrison had quickly summoned to defend the town almost 800 militiamen.

For three days, the livid Shawnee chief refused to meet with the Indiana Territory governor. But on July 30, he finally relented. "He said," Harrison wrote to Eustis, "that after much trouble and difficulty he had at length brought all the northern tribes to unite and place themselves under his direction… As soon as the council was over he was to set out on a visit to the southern tribes to get them to unite with those of the North." And when he returned, Tecumseh had promised, "he would then go and see the president and settle everything with him."

On August 4, the Shawnee chief rode south with Shabbona, the Creek shaman Seekaboo, a Creek guide, and 16 Shawnees, Potawatomis, and Winnebagos. To impress the southern Indians, all had replaced their usual tribal dress with a common uniform. From otherwise shaved heads, encircled by silver bands on red flannel strips, fell three plaits of hair dressed with hawk feathers. All had painted small red dots across their foreheads, red half-circles beneath their eyes, and large red dots in the centers of their chests. All wore the same buckskin hunting shirts, loincloths, and fringed leggings, with silver bands around their arms above the elbows and around their wrists. Tecumseh alone wore a mark of distinction, an eagle feather died red and white that rose from the front of his silver headband.

The Shawnee, Harrison wrote to Eustis, "is one of those uncommon geniuses which spring up occasionally to produce revolutions and overthrow the established order of things." Such men, the Indiana Territory governor knew, must be able to inspire fanatical loyalty. "The implicit obedience and respect which the followers of Tecumseh pay to him," he wrote, "is really astonishing."

But such men also must be masters of darker arts. After Tecumseh's party had left, Harrison had watched the Indians from Prophetstown who had not followed Tecumseh south. "Although the greater part of his followers are attached to him from principle and affection," he wrote, "there are many of them who follow him through fear; and he was scarcely a mile from the town before they indulged in the most virulent invectives against him."

The Indian chief who confronted Tecumseh probably was the Miami Deaf Man (Shepoconah), whose wife was Frances Slocum (Moconnoquah). As a five-year-old girl, she had been taken by raiding Delawares in 1778 near Wilkes-Barre, Pennsylvania. Fifty-nine years later, two of her brothers found her, and commissioned this 1839 George Winter portrait of their lost sister. (Courtesy of the Tippecanoe County Historical Association, Lafayette, Indiana.)

This 1813 portrait by Rembrandt Peale depicts William Henry Harrison. (Author's collection)

This engraving from Lossing's *Pictorial Field-Book of the War of 1812* depicts John Parke Boyd. (Author's collection)

Harrison now had seen two Tecumsehs. The Shawnee who had visited in 1810, he thought, had been so possessed by his vision that he had spoken of what remained to be achieved as if it already had been accomplished. But he also had wanted peace.

This Tecumseh, Harrison judged, was already at war. An enemy still too weak to strike, he had broken his promise to attain some end by deceit. "I have not been able to determine what was the object of Tecumseh coming here with so large a force," he wrote to Eustis, "That he had some design in mind which he thought fit to abandon is most evident."

Barron then reported a curious incident. While he had been talking with Tecumseh in Vincennes, a chief visiting the Indiana Territory capital had accosted the Shawnee. He had learned, the chief shouted at Tecumseh, that the Shawnee was planning to kill him. "Come and kill me," he continued, waving his tomahawk and screaming insults, "You and your men can kill the white people's hogs and call them bears, but you dare not face a warrior." To Barron's astonishment, Tecumseh had sat silent, ignoring the taunts until the man left.

"My spies," Harrison reported to Eustis, "say that he intended to demand a retraction of the late purchase, and if it was not obtained, determined to seize some of the chiefs who were active in making the treaty in my presence and put them to death." Whatever Tecumseh's plan had been, the Indiana Territory governor's action had thwarted it. But he could not maintain at Vincennes indefinitely a force capable of defending the town against a surprise attack. The Indians at Prophetstown must be dispersed.

Two days after the Shawnee's departure, a relieved Harrison learned from Eustis that Col. John Parke Boyd's 4th US Infantry Regiment was on its way from Pittsburgh. "Tecumseh," Harrison wrote to Eustis on August 7, "is now upon the last round to put a finishing stroke to his work. I hope, however, before his return, that that part of the fabric which he considered complete will be demolished, and even its foundation rooted up."

FROM VINCENNES TO FORT HARRISON

While Tecumseh was away, Harrison had decided, he would lead an army to Prophetstown. The Indiana Territory governor had never commanded an army, nor even a small unit in battle. But as an aide to Wayne, he

The advance to Fort Harrison

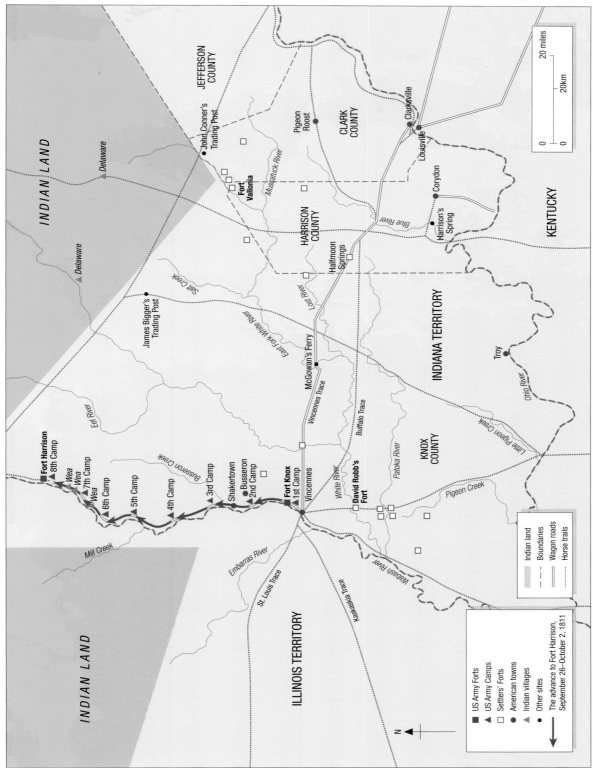

Pushmataha would die in 1824 while visiting Washington, and be buried in the Congressional Cemetery with the rank of a US Army brigadier-general. He was, said Andrew Jackson, "the greatest and bravest Indian I ever knew." This 2001 portrait by Katherine Roche Buchanan depicts the Choctaw chief. (Courtesy of Mississippi Department of Archives and History)

had watched the great commander devise and execute a plan for just such a mission as he now would undertake.

When Eustis had dispatched the 4th US Infantry Regiment in response to Harrison's plea, he had said that Prophetstown was not to be attacked unless such action proved "absolutely necessary." The Indiana Territory governor had responded with a request that Eustis expressly authorize such an attack if the Indians there would not disperse. But even if he failed to receive such permission in time, Harrison thought, the Indians would justify such action by themselves attacking his army as it advanced.

Harrison did not underestimate the danger his army would face. As an 18-year-old ensign, he had seen the shattered remnant of the first US Army return from Wabash to Cincinnati. No American army, he knew, had ever defeated in a significant engagement an Indian army it did not greatly outnumber.

He would need, Harrison thought, an army of at least a thousand. And though it would lack artillery, it otherwise would resemble as closely as possible Wayne's at Fallen Timbers. "The event of General Wayne's action," he wrote to Eustis, "proved that disciplined musketry with their flanks secured by dragoons and mounted riflemen are the best troops against Indians."

Boyd's regulars would provide the disciplined musketry. Indiana Territory militiamen would add to their numbers. Harrison sent orders to the closest of the territory's seven counties, instructing the Clark, Harrison, and Knox County militia commanders to dispatch companies to join the regulars in Vincennes by September 22.

The sparsely populated Indiana Territory, however, could not provide dragoons and mounted riflemen in sufficient numbers. Harrison asked Kentucky Governor Charles Scott, who had led 1,500 horsemen at Fallen Timbers, for permission to recruit volunteer dragoons and mounted riflemen in the neighboring state.

Harrison also was acutely aware of the logistical difficulties he would face in a campaign in the wilderness. St Clair's army had almost starved before reaching Wabash, and Wayne's while returning from Fallen Timbers. St Clair's, moreover, had lacked many types of essential supplies.

Soon, Vincennes was the center of a frenzy of activity as Harrison's aides and contractors began assembling what the army would need. From the territorial armory came powder and balls, buckshot, and paper for cartridges. From the local mills came sacks of flour for the bread Harrison's men would eat. From merchants and farms came oxen for the herd that would advance with the army to provide beef; horses to carry supplies; and watercraft and wagons to carry still more.

As the army's supplies accumulated at Vincennes, Indiana Territory militia companies began to form for Harrison's campaign. In Clark County, Lt. Col. Joseph Bartholomew summoned to Charlestown Capt. John Norris's musket company, Capt. James Bigger's rifle company, and Capt. Charles Beggs' dragoon troop. In Harrison County, Capt. Spier Spencer mustered in Corydon his mounted rifle company, and Capts. Thomas Berry's and Zachariah Lindley's smaller companies. In Knox County, Lt. Col. Luke Decker assembled in Vincennes the musket companies of Capts. Walter Wilson, Jacob Warrick, William Hargrove, Andrew Wilkins, and Thomas Scott; and Capt. Benjamin Parke's dragoon troop.

Harrison then went to Kentucky. When Boyd's 4th US Infantry Regiment reached Louisville on August 31, Harrison was there recruiting Kentucky volunteers. On September 4, he and Boyd returned to Vincennes to plan the campaign.

Like Harrison, Boyd had begun his military career as a US Army ensign. But Boyd had resigned his commission to become a mercenary in India. In 1790, he had become an officer in the army of the Nizam of Hyderabad, which had, Boyd wrote to his father, 150,000 infantry, 60,000 cavalry, and 500 elephants. His first command had been a unit larger than the army that would advance to Prophetstown. He had then fought for nearly 20 years in the wars of the British and their native allies against Tipu Sultan and the Mahratta Confederacy. Now, the dismayed Boyd learned, he was to fight under a commander who had never led men against an enemy.

As Harrison and Boyd awaited the arrival of the army, Tecumseh and his party moved south. Their destination was the largest Creek town, Tuckabatchee, near present Tallassee, Alabama. There a great council of Chickasaw, Choctaw, Cherokee, and Creek chiefs was to convene in September with the American Indian agent Benjamin Hawkins.

On their way to Tuckabatchee, the northern Indians visited the principal Chickasaw and Choctaw towns. The Chickasaws were ancient enemies of the Ohio Indians, who had sent warriors to aid St Clair and Wayne. Raiding between the enemies had ceased only in 1797, when the Americans had negotiated a peace. From the Chickasaws, Tecumseh received a chilly reception.

Cut by George Rogers Clark for his 1786 campaign against the Indians, the Vincennes Trace followed for most of its first 35 miles the famous Buffalo Trace, an Indian trail that tracked a buffalo migration route. This surviving section of the road is near Palmyra, Indiana. (Author's collection)

It grew worse when the northern Indians reached the Choctaws. At first, many warriors responded favorably to Tecumseh's speeches. But then came another voice. At 13, Pushmataha had won fame as a warrior in his first battle against the Creeks. At 20, he had won his name, the Bringer of Death, by taking in a single battle five Osage scalps. Rising and facing Tecumseh, the greatest of Choctaw chiefs said "I know your history well. You have always been a troublemaker… When you have found yourself unable to pick a quarrel with the white man, you have stirred up strife between different tribes of your own race… Not only that, you are a monarch and unyielding tyrant within your own domain. Every Shawnee man, woman and child must bow in humble submission to your imperious will."

On September 12, the Clark and Harrison County units began marching toward Half Moon Spring, where they were to rendezvous. Bartholomew's Clark County men marched west from Clarksville on the Vincennes Trace. Spencer's Harrison County men rode forward from Corydon on a horse trail to Harrison's Spring, where the territorial governor had an estate and mill. Then they followed another horse trail north to the Vincennes Trace.

On September 14, when the Clark and Harrison County units met at Half Moon Spring, the first Kentuckians left Louisville. After crossing the Ohio River, Capt. Peter Funk led his troop of 30 dragoons along the Vincennes Trace. With him rode six Kentuckians who had volunteered to serve in any capacity in which they would be useful. They included the famous lawyer Joseph Daviess, the US Attorney for Kentucky; and George Rogers Clark's 19-year-old nephew George Croghan.

When the Kentuckians reached Vincennes, Funk received a captain's commission in the Indiana Territory militia. Daviess, who became a major, was given command of the army's dragoon squadron. Croghan found a position as an aide-de-camp to Boyd.

Soon another volunteer arrived, Daviess's old friend Isaac White. A colonel in the new Illinois Territory militia, he had been unable to bring his regiment. But he'd come himself to serve as a private in Parke's dragoon troop. As a symbol of their friendship, Daviess and White exchanged swords.

On the evening of September 19, Boyd's 4th Regiment regulars ended their 1,022-mile-long river journey to Vincennes. "It was dark before we landed," wrote Adam Walker of Lt. Abraham Hawkins' US Rifle Regiment company, "and by the noise and confusion about us, we concluded the town to be overrun with troops. A rabble soon gathered about the boats and assisted in hauling them ashore. Their whooping and yells, and their appearance caused us to doubt whether we had not actually landed among the savages themselves."

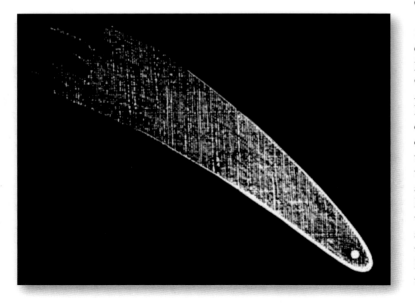

Tecumseh's "Shooting Star," the Great Comet of 1811, created wide excitement across North America and Europe. In Russia, wrote Leo Tolstoy in *War and Peace*, it "was said to portend all kinds of woes and the end of the world." This 19th-century engraving reproduced a drawing of the comet by the British astronomer and antiquary William Henry Smyth. (Author's collection)

As the American regulars were landing, Tecumseh's party arrived at Tuckabatchee. Despite his humiliating reception by the Chickasaws, the Shawnee remained confident. Now he would be with his mother's people, the Creeks. His mother, he had told Ruddell, had named him Tecumseh, the "Shooting Star," for a light that had raced across the heavens on the night of his birth. And now, as a sign of the Great Spirit's approval of his mission, a great Shooting Star had appeared in the night sky.

On September 20, Tecumseh and the northern Indians waited until sunset to make a dramatic appearance at Hawkins' council. With faces painted black, eagle feathers rising from their headbands, and stiff buffalo tails hanging from their belts and extending from bands around their arms, they arrived just as the day's talk was ending. After parading around the council site several times, they shook hands with the assembled chiefs and gave them gifts of tobacco.

For the next eight days, Tecumseh sat at the council in silence, listening to Hawkins and the southern chiefs. Finally the American Indian agent asked him whether he had come to recruit allies for a war against the Americans. "The Indians," Tecumseh responded, "should unite in peace and friendship among themselves and cultivate the same with their white neighbors."

But after each day's sunset, Tecumseh's Shooting Star reappeared. And below the great, long-tailed light, Creek warriors watched with delight as Tecumseh and his party performed the war dance of the Shawnee. To the beat of a drum, the singing northern Indians marched in unison solemnly around a post. Then each in turn leapt forward to attack it with his tomahawk, shouting of his deeds in prior battles. Soon Creek warriors were joining in what they called "the dance of the lakes."

As the Indians talked and danced in Tuckabatchee, Harrison reviewed his march, encampment, and battle plans with his officers. The army, he explained, would advance about 70 miles to a site on the east bank of the Wabash known as Bataille des Illinois. There, where the Iroquois had fought a great 17th-century battle against the Illinois Indians, the Americans would build a fort. Then they would advance to Prophetstown.

Behind pioneers felling trees for the road that would carry the army's wagons, the main body would march up the east bank of the Wabash. Between two columns of regulars and militiamen, the wagons, cattle, horses, and senior officers would advance on the road. Mounted riflemen and dragoons would form a screen around the army, providing advance, rear, and flank guards. Watercraft would carry additional supplies up the river, as more mounted riflemen guarded the west bank of the Wabash.

This drawing by Adam Walker shows the order of march of Harrison's army from Vincennes. (Author's collection)

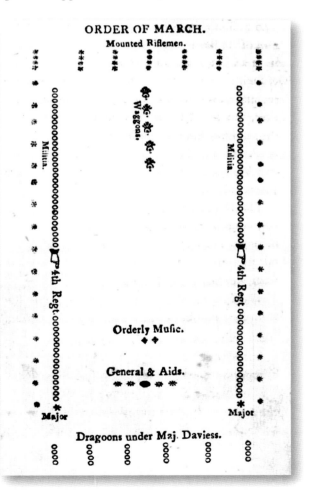

ORDER OF MARCH.

The army would camp in rectangles, with the right column as the long front side, and the left the rear. The mounted and foot rifle companies would camp on the short sides. The dragoons would remain in the center, where they would serve as a reserve in case of attack.

The Indians, Harrison explained, usually attacked at dawn. The army therefore would awaken at least an hour before the first light. The captains would form their soldiers into battle lines five steps ahead of their tents or other sleeping locations, and remain in the position until full daylight. Their cartridges, he added, would contain buckshot rather than balls, which would be more effective in a battle with the Indians.

"The governor will command in person," an impressed Lt. Charles Larrabee wrote to his cousin Adam. And, the young officer added, he seemed to know what he was doing. Harrison was, he wrote, "a firm man and a very good disciplinarian and acquainted with the Indian fighting, which is different from all others."

On September 22, the Indiana Territory governor was ready to lead his army forward. After parading through the streets of Vincennes before its commander's review, it marched 3 miles to its 1st Camp, near Fort Knox. There Harrison continued to prepare his officers and soldiers for what was to come. He explained to them, wrote Larrabee, "the maneuvers of Indian warfare."

And, to the astonishment of all, the Indiana Territory governor made it clear who now commanded the 4th US Infantry Regiment. After reviewing all punishments ordered by noncommissioned officers, he won his soldiers' hearts by summarily canceling those that were not justified. "All kinds of petty punishments, inflicted without authority, for the most trifling errors of the private soldier, by the pompous sergeant, or the insignificant corporal," wrote a gleeful Walker, "were at once prohibited."

As Harrison made his final preparations to advance, many Indian chiefs appeared at the Americans' 1st Camp. His army soon would march, Harrison told them. They should tell Tenskwatawa that he must appear at a council immediately, surrender all warriors who had attacked Americans, and return all stolen horses and other property. When five Delaware chiefs offered to arrange the council, Harrison sent them forward to Prophetstown on September 24.

On September 26, Harrison's 1,200-man army moved north up the east bank of the Wabash. Major George Rogers Clark Floyd, the commandant of Fort Knox, led the right column and William Baen, the senior 4th Regiment

This truncated stockade traces the outline of Fort Knox at Ouabache Trails Park near Vincennes. (Author's collection)

captain, the left. Two pirogues carried the army's heavy supplies on the river as Spencer's horsemen rode up its west bank. "Scarce a row of sober faces is to be seen with the 4th Infantry," Larrabee wrote, "on account of being now pleased." After a march of 10 miles, the army halted at its 2nd Camp.

On September 27, the Americans passed through the last American settlement, Shakertown, built two years before by 400 Shakers. Then they crossed into the land the Indians had ceded in 1809. After a 10-mile march, they halted at their 3rd Camp.

On September 28, Harrison's army advanced another 10 miles to its 4th camp. That day, Hawkins ended his council at Tuckabatchee and departed. Then Tecumseh's council began. He had not lied to Hawkins, he said. He wanted peace. But first there would be war. The Indians would fight with the support of the Great Spirit. From the Great Lakes to the Gulf of Mexico, they all should fight together, and draw in blood a final boundary to American settlement.

While Tecumseh argued in Tuckabatchee, Harrison's army continued its march north. Advancing about 10 miles a day, it halted briefly at its 5th through 7th Camps, On October 2, it reached at last Bataille des Illinois, the site of its 8th Camp. The next day, Larrabee recalled, "At half after 7:00 A. M. the whole army were drawn up in solid columns, and a speech was delivered by the commander in chief informing that a fort would be built here."

Harrison then watched his axemen begin felling trees for construction rather than road clearing. When the army marched again, he knew, the road building would be easier. For much of their route to Prophetstown would be on flatter ground, through grassland rather than forest.

For a thousand miles, the great woods reached west from the Atlantic coast of New England, spanning the Appalachian Mountains, the Ohio River, and the Great Lakes. In Ohio and Kentucky, there sometimes were small areas of prairie, surrounded by forest. But now the prairies were growing so large that the woods were becoming the islands. "When the traveler enters the prairie from the woods," wrote Larrabee, "he beholds with astonishment a cleared piece of land extending from 6 to 15 miles in length, from 1 to 7 in breadth clothed with wild grass which makes good hay for stock cattle."

The prairie, he added, was "as clear of trees, roots or brush as any mowing lot in the Yankee states is." The grassland offered little wood for the campfires the Americans needed to cook and keep warm. On October 4, Harrison sent men to collect an alternative fuel. "Found thirty men commanded by Lt. McMahon," Pvt. John Tipton of Spencer's company wrote in his journal, "was to guard a boat going to the Vermilion River for coal. I went with them."

On October 7, McMahon's men returned with a large supply. But they found at the Americans' 8th Camp dissatisfaction. "Some men," Tipton wrote in his journal, "wants to go home."

George Rogers Clark Floyd wore this coat at Tippecanoe. It is now displayed at Locust Grove, a museum in Louisville. (Graphic Enterprises)

FROM FORT HARRISON TO PROPHETSTOWN

It was dangerous, Harrison knew, to halt an advancing army for long. But he lacked sufficient food to go any farther forward. Despite his efforts, the army's contractors had failed to supply enough flour by the time the army had marched north. Pirogues, he had been promised, soon would arrive with more.

While the army remained at its 8th Camp, its numbers would diminish. Illness would claim some. When armies assembled, soldiers arrived with disease. The 4th Regiment had carried with it from Pittsburgh some debilitating sickness. Of the 500 men who had descended the Ohio, only 350 had marched north from Vincennes.

Idleness and boredom would claim others. Many of the militiamen had enlisted expecting a short campaign. As their excitement at beginning the adventure faded, there would be desertions. And every day, the numbers leaving would rise. "Some murmuring took place among them," wrote Walker, "being heartily sick of the camp, and desirous of returning to their homes. Many, indeed, threatened to leave us at all hazards, which caused the governor much anxiety and trouble."

Still more would go back down the road to Vincennes, if Harrison had to reduce the soldiers' daily flour rations. To delay such action, he sent men to find another source of food. From abandoned Indian fields, they gathered corn that could be ground to provide a substitute for wheat flour. But few liked the cornbread it produced.

The men not working on the fort were allowed to hunt and fish. To the delight of New England regulars like Larrabee, the westerners soon were "seen coming into camp with deer and honey, both of which this part of the world abounds in." "There was caught in the river here," the astonished lieutenant wrote, "a catfish which weighed 122 lbs."

Those not building the fort also received training in how to maneuver in battle. At Fallen Timbers, the American commander had seen how the ability of Wayne's soldiers to move quickly to assigned battle positions had made the difference between victory and defeat. To enable his units to deploy more efficiently, he abandoned the usual American practice of forming in double rank. "In the formation of my troops I used a single rank, or what was called 'Indian file,'" he would write to Eustis. "Raw troops maneuver with much more facility in single rather than double rank."

But every day, there were fewer to maneuver. His army, Harrrison realized, would have to be reinforced. He had his captains send messengers back to the areas in which they had recruited to urge new men to enlist to fill their units' depleted ranks. He asked Knox County Capt. David Robb to assemble as quickly as possible another mounted rifle company. He dispatched Floyd to Brig. Gen. Samuel Wells, the commander of the Louisville units of the Kentucky militia, and brother of the Fort Wayne Indian agent. Wells, Harrison asked, should send immediately as many mounted riflemen as he could find.

This colored lithograph from Mckenney and Hall reproduces Charles Bird King's 1828 portrait of Sequoya. In 1811, Sequoya was attempting to devise a method of written communication for the Cherokees. He ultimately developed the script shown in the portrait, in which signs represented the syllables of Cherokee words. (Author's collection)

The Advance to Prophetstown

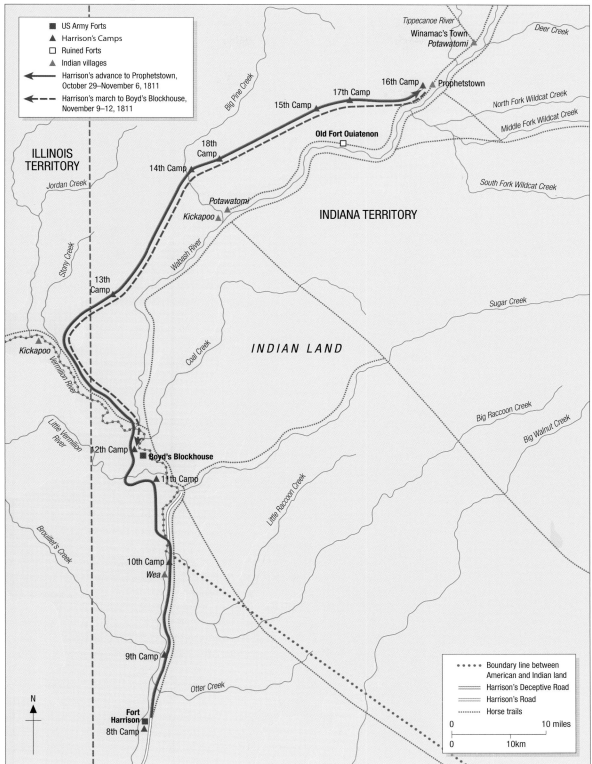

Legend:
- US Army Forts
- Harrison's Camps
- Ruined Forts
- Indian villages
- Harrison's advance to Prophetstown, October 29–November 6, 1811
- Harrison's march to Boyd's Blockhouse, November 9–12, 1811

Tippecanoe River
Deer Creek
Winamac's Town
Potawatomi
16th Camp
Prophetstown
17th Camp
15th Camp
North Fork Wildcat Creek
Big Pine Creek
Middle Fork Wildcat Creek
18th Camp
Old Fort Ouiatenon
14th Camp
ILLINOIS TERRITORY
Jordan Creek
South Fork Wildcat Creek
Potawatomi
Kickapoo
INDIANA TERRITORY
Stony Creek
Wabash River
13th Camp
Sugar Creek
INDIAN LAND
Kickapoo
Coal Creek
Vermillion River
Big Raccoon Creek
Little Vermillion River
Big Walnut Creek
12th Camp
Boyd's Blockhouse
11th Camp
Little Raccoon Creek
10th Camp
Wea
Brouillet's Creek
9th Camp
N
Otter Creek
Fort Harrison
8th Camp

Legend:
- Boundary line between American and Indian land
- Harrison's Deceptive Road
- Harrison's Road
- Horse trails

0 — 10 miles
0 — 10km

53

Five hundred miles to the south, the Tuckabatchee council had ended in disappointment for Tecumseh. Like the Chickasaws and Choctaws, the Cherokees said that they wanted no part of what he planned. Tecumseh should go home, said Sequoya and the tribe's other chiefs. And if he and his northern Indians tried to visit Cherokee villages, the chiefs warned, they would be killed.

The Creek chiefs too had rejected his proposal, but, despite the disapproval of men like the great Creek chief William McIntosh, the Shawnee and his party lingered on after the end of the council. Instead of returning north, they commenced a tour of the tribe's villages. There, as Tecumseh addressed crowds of warriors, Seekaboo supervised the construction of structures where Creek converts could shake hands with the Prophet.

At Prophetstown, Tenskwatawa was unsure how to respond to Harrison's advance. His brother had left strict orders that there was to be no fighting while he was gone. But the appearance of Tecumseh's Shooting Star had excited the Indians at his village. To distract them, the Shawnee shaman had ordered the construction of elaborate log breastworks around Prophetstown. But finally the clamor for action against the Americans had grown too great to resist. A small party, he announced, should go to the American camp, take prisoners, and bring them back to be tortured to death.

Several Shawnee warriors then went south to capture the victims. On October 10, they reached Harrison's 8th Camp. At 8.00pm, an American sentinel detected one creeping forward in the darkness. "An Indian," Walker recalled, "crept cautiously through the bushes, opposite one of the sentinels in the main guard and shot him through both thighs. The sentinel nearest to him saw the flash of the rifle, and immediately presented his piece, snapped it twice. Both times it missed fire! The Indian made his escape, the camp was alarmed, and the troops called to arms."

Harrison's training of his men then produced impressive results. The Americans, Larrabee remembered, "in 25 seconds were paraded in the line of encampment, which was the line of battle for a night attack." "The dragoons," Walker recalled, "were instantly formed, and under the command of that gallant and spirited officer, Major Daviess, sallied out, and scoured the woods in the vicinity of the encampment; but no Indians could be found… We stood to our arms the whole of this night, while the governor and Col. Boyd were riding down the lines animating the troops to do their duty in case we were attacked."

For the next five nights, gunshots in the woods around the camp awakened the Americans. At the same time, Indians professing friendship began to appear every day. The first were Delawares, who arrived on October 11. "One," Tipton wrote in his journal on October 12, "spoke good English. Played cards with the men." "They all," Larrabee recalled, "appeared to be friendly, (but want good looking to) and said they did not intend to join the Prophet, but had tried to dissuade him and his party not to go to war against the white people."

On October 18, the American commander received a letter from Eustis expressly authorizing the course of action he had planned to follow. "After advancing to the Prophet's village," Eustis had written on September 18, "You will approach and order him to disperse, which he may be permitted to do… If he neglects or refuses to disperse he will be attacked and compelled to it by the force under your command."

At 7.30am the following morning, Harrison addressed his assembled officers and soldiers. He told them, Tipton wrote in his journal, "that we should have to fight the Indians." But their commander also had less welcome news. There still was insufficient flour to advance. And the Americans now would have only three-quarter flour rations.

While Harrison was speaking, the weather turned. "It began," Tipton wrote, "to rain. We were dismissed. It rained hard to sunset… It stopped raining and began to snow and blow hard. Our camp smoked. It was the disagreeablest night I ever saw."

The bad weather continued. "A very cold, cloudy day, ground covered with snow," Tipton wrote on October 20. But as deserters marched south through the mud toward Vincennes, they began to encounter reinforcements arriving in response to Harrison's pleas. "Six men run away," Tipton wrote on October 25, "and six men came to camp today."

Encouraged by news that flour and more reinforcements were on their way, the American commander now began the last stage of his soldiers' training. To prepare his men for what they would face, Wayne had had them fight mock battles with frontiersmen dressed as Indians. Now the woods around Harrison's camp echoed for two days with the sounds of American soldiers fighting American warriors.

On October 27, the Delaware emissaries Harrison had sent to Prophetstown on September 24 finally returned. Treated like prisoners, and threatened with execution, they had at last been released. There were about 450 warriors at Tenskwatawa's village, they reported, and more were arriving every day. And they had seen a warrior tell a pleased Tenskwatawa that he'd shot a guard at the American camp.

That same day, Harrison assembled the army to celebrate the completion of the fort. "I christen this Fort Harrison," shouted Daviess, smashing a bottle of whiskey on the gate. But one of the Kentuckians, Funk remembered, disapproved. "It's too bad," he said, "to waste whiskey that way. Water would have done just as well."

On October 28, Robb rode into the camp with a company of about 60 Knox County mounted riflemen. Two pirogues and three keelboats arrived as well. They brought only enough flour for a few days. But three more keelboats with flour, they told Harrison, were only a few days behind.

Unwilling to wait any longer, the American commander ordered the army to proceed on half rations to the mouth of the Vermilion River. There, as his men waited for the keelboats, they would build a blockhouse as an advanced supply base. Supplies delivered while they were advancing to Prophetstown would await them there when they returned.

On October 29, the Americans at last marched north from their 8th Camp leaving Lt. Col. James Miller and 100

On September 4–5, 1812, about 600 Indians would attack Fort Harrison. Captain Zachary Taylor's company, which Lt. Jacob Albright had led at Tippecanoe, would successfully repel them. This engraving from Lossing's *Field-Book of the War of 1812* shows the appearance of the fort in what is now Terre Haute, Indiana. (Author's collection)

men at Fort Harrison. "The army is not as large as when it left Vincennes," wrote Larrabee. But the departures had created opportunities for some. When one of Spencer's officers had left, Tipton had been elected the company's ensign. Now, he wrote in his journal, the army consisted of "about 640 foot, 270 mounted men, 19 wagons and 1 cart."

As Harrison's army cautiously advanced 5 miles to its 9th Camp, a party of Delaware and Miami chiefs accompanied the Americans. Despite the treatment of the prior Delaware emissaries, they had volunteered to carry a message from Harrison to Tenskwatawa. Prophetstown, they were to say, could remain as a Shawnee village, but the other Indians there must disperse.

On October 30, when Harrison's army advanced another 8 miles to its 10th Camp, the Delaware and Miami chiefs went ahead. The trail led up the east bank of the Wabash. But Prophetstown was on the west bank. Travelers usually crossed the river at the mouth of Big Pine Creek, from where a trail led to Prophetstown, or crossed to the trail opposite the site of the old French Fort Ouiatenon.

The American axemen, the Indians expected, would cut their road along the east bank of the Wabash until the Americans forded the river at one of those points. But his army, Harrison decided, would instead cross the Wabash immediately. It then would advance by a roundabout course through the prairie far beyond the river. Although the route would be longer, the terrain would allow his pioneers to cut their road with little effort. It also would provide an ample supply of grass for the army's horses. And, if the Americans moved rapidly, they might reach Prophetstown without detection.

In 1794, Harrison had watched Wayne deceive Indian scouts on the St Marys River in Ohio. After building a road in one direction, he had led his army in another. Now Harrison would conceal his crossing of the Wabash in the same way. On October 31, the army's axemen went forward on the trail, cutting their road as far as Coal Creek. But, as they labored, the Americans began fording the Wabash 5 miles behind them.

After three hours spent crossing the river, the Americans marched another 7 miles before halting at their 11th Camp. "We took a north course up the east side of the Wabash and crossed to the west," Tilton wrote in his journal, "with orders to kill all the Indians we saw. Fine news."

Before the day ended, more reinforcements arrived at the 11th Camp. Samuel Wells had come himself with Frederick Geiger, a Kentucky militia colonel and 60 mounted riflemen. Harrison immediately appointed Wells an Indiana Territory major, and gave him command of the army's mounted rifle units. Geiger became an Indiana Territory captain. And among Geiger's men Harrison found an old friend, Kentucky militia Col. Abraham Owen, who had enlisted in Geiger's unit as a private. Harrison appointed him an aide-de-camp.

This Samuel F. B. Morse portrait depicts James Miller. After promotion to brigadier-general during the War of 1812, he would in 1819 become the first governor of the Arkansas Territory. (Courtesy of the Arkansas Governor's Mansion and the Arkansas Arts Center Foundation Collection: Purchase, Samuel F. B. Morse Acquisition Fund)

On November 1, Harrison's army moved across the Little Vermilion River into the swampy area around the mouth of the Vermilion. There it was necessary to build a log road for the wagons. After advancing about 3 miles, it halted at its 12th Camp on the Wabash. Three keelboats then arrived with enough flour to allow the army to advance farther on half rations.

The day before, the boatmen reported, there had been an Indian attack near Fort Harrison. After the failed Shawnee attempt to take prisoners, the Potawatomi Wabaunsee had led a party south from Prophetstown to take scalps. On October 31, a target had presented itself. Wabaunsee had swum out to a keelboat on the Wabash, where he had tomahawked and scalped a man aboard.

On November 2, Harrison's men built the advanced base at the end of their water supply route. A 25-foot-square blockhouse with breastworks extending to the Wabash, the Americans named it Boyd's Blockhouse. The following day, they crossed the Vermilion, marched far up the stream, and then moved northeast into the prairie. Eager to get to Prophetstown before their ruse was discovered, they advanced 18 miles to their 13th Camp.

This colored lithograph from McKenney and Hall reproduced Charles Bird King's 1835 portrait of Wabaunsee. (Author's collection)

On November 4, as the Americans advanced another 18 miles to Big Pine Creek, the site of their 14th Camp, the Prophetstown warriors continued to demand an attack on Harrison's approaching army. Unaware that the Americans were marching across the western prairie, their commanders recommended attacking them as they crossed the Wabash.

The growing pressure on the Shawnee shaman to disobey Tecumseh's orders then was relieved by the arrival of the Delaware and Miami chiefs sent

These reconstructed Indian structures are at the site of Tenskwatawa's village, now Prophetstown State Park. (Photograph by Jonathan Winkler)

by Harrison. Eager to delay any confrontation with the Americans, Tenskwatawa sent them back to Harrison with emissaries. Harrison, they were to say, should stop his advance. The Prophet then would come to the place where he halted for a peace council.

On November 5, the Delaware and Miami chiefs, and Tenskwatawa's emissaries, rushed south to find the American commander. As they moved south on the east bank of the Wabash, Harrison's army marched another 18 miles to its 15th Camp. Prophetstown, Dubois's scouts said, now was about 12 miles ahead.

At sunrise on November 6, the Americans went forward again. They moved cautiously, expecting to be attacked at any moment. After advancing about 8 miles, they halted at 1.00pm. There the men removed their knapsacks, which were left in the wagons with the cattle and a guard.

The Americans then advanced another mile and halted again. After their roundabout march across the prairie, they now had returned to the Wabash. But instead of the flat terrain the American commander had expected, ahead lay wooded ridges and ravines. His scouts, the furious Harrison complained, had led the army "onto ground so broken and disadvantageous to us that I was obliged to change the position of the troops several times in the course of a mile."

Behind the scouts and Daviess's dragoons, Harrison deployed his units to respond to an ambush. The companies advancing on foot moved apart into separate single-file columns, at distances that would allow them to form a battle line quickly. The columns of mounted riflemen on the flanks formed to go forward in five lines. Then, remembered Larrabee, "The march was slow, in order that the scouting parties might have time to examine all the places where it was likely Indians might be secreted… The several corps had to change positions 3 or 4 times as the situation of the ground presented itself."

After emerging from the difficult ground unscathed, the Americans continued to advance. About a mile from Prophetstown, they were seen by Indians, who raced back to the village to give the alarm. About a half-mile farther, Harrison's men came in sight of the great cornfields that extended around Tenskwatawa's village. There the army halted again. Harrison ordered Floyd to form the infantry companies marching on the right into a front battle line, and Baen to form those on the left into a rear line. Wells' two mounted rifle companies formed on the left flank, and Spencer's on the right.

The high ground upon which the Americans camped, as seen from Prophetstown. (Photograph by Jonathan Winkler)

Then the lines went forward. After a few hundred yards, Prophetstown itself came into view. "The Indians," remembered Walker, "appeared much surprised and terrified at our sudden appearance before their town. We perceived them running in every direction about the village, apparently in great confusion. Their object, however, was to regain in season their different positions behind a breastwork of logs which encircled the town from the bank of the Wabash." Tenskwatawa's Indians, Harrison recalled, "had fortified their town with care and astonishing labor for them."

Three warriors with a white flag then appeared. Emissaries from Tenskwatawa, they told Harrison, shortly would arrive to meet with him. About 150 yards from Prophetstown, Harrison halted the army to await them. "In this situation," remembered Larrabee, "the army and town were in full view of each other."

As the Americans waited for the emissaries, Harrison talked with his senior officers. All wanted to attack Prophetstown immediately. His orders, Harrison responded, did not allow him to attack until the Indians had refused to abandon the village.

A delegation of three chiefs then arrived to meet with the American commander. Tenskwatawa, they said, had sent emissaries back with the Delaware and Miami chiefs to assure the Americans that he wanted peace. Harrison's early crossing of the Wabash, they said, had caused him to miss them. The three chiefs, Walker recalled, begged Harrison "not to proceed to open hostilities; but to encamp with the troops for that night. And in the morning, they solemnly promised to come into camp and hold a council and they would agree to almost any terms the governor might propose."

While the American commander talked with the Indians, Larrabee remembered, he and his men waited in their battle lines "about half an hour." After Tenskwatawa's emissaries returned to Prophetstown, Walker recalled, Harrison told his officers that they had agreed that "no hostilities should be committed on either side till after an interview tomorrow." Harrison then sent several officers to inspect ground that the Indians had recommended as campsite.

The American officers, Walker remembered, "returned with a favorable report of the place." Harrison then ordered the wagons and cattle brought forward to join the army. As a drizzling rain began to fall, the Americans marched to the site where they would camp, about three-quarters of a mile west of Prophetstown.

THE BATTLE OF TIPPECANOE

When the sun set at 5.40pm, the Americans were at the site of their 16th Camp, a 500-yard-long, oak-covered ridge. Pointing toward the southwest, it narrowed as it descended about 30 feet from high ground. To the west flowed Burnett Creek. To the east, beyond about 1,400 yards of marsh and prairie, was Prophetstown.

The Americans' camp had two 300-yard-long sides upon which they could form battle lines facing Tenskwatawa's village. On their left flank, the front line would be about 150 yards ahead of the rear. On the right, on ground about 10 feet lower, it would be only about 80 yards ahead of the rear line.

As rain fell, the Americans occupied the locations where they would sleep, which were about 3–4 yards behind their assigned positions in the battle lines. The US Army men would be in tents. Commissioned officers had their own, and two noncommissioned officers, or six soldiers, shared the others. Some of the militia officers also had tents, like a large one that Geiger had brought with him from Kentucky. But the other militiamen would sleep in lean-tos they had built of branches and bark, or lie rolled in blankets.

About 285 men armed with muskets were in two battalions on the front side of the camp. On the left were the 205 men of Maj. George Rogers Clark Boyd's six-company Front Line US Infantry Battalion. At its far left, at the camp's northeastern corner, was Lt. Abraham Hawkins' 30-man company. To their right were the 40-man companies of Lt. Charles Larrabee, Capt. Josiah Snelling, and Capt. George Prescott. Then came Lt. Jacob Albright's 20 men, and Capt. Return Brown's 35. Beyond the regulars were about 80 men in Lt. Col. Joseph Bartholomew's two-company Front Line Indiana Territory Militia Battalion. Captains Andrew Wilkins and Thomas Scott led its 40-man companies.

Another 325 musket men were in two battalions on the camp's rear side. On the right, as the side faced out from the camp, were about 120 regulars in Capt. William Baen's three-company Rear Line US Infantry Battalion. At its far right, at the camp's northwestern corner, was Capt. Robert Barton's 40-man company. Next came the 40-man companies of Capt. Joel Cook and Lt. George Peters. To Peters' left were the about 205 men of Lt. Col. Luke Decker's four-company Rear Line Indiana Territory Militia Battalion. First came the 55 men in Capt. William Hargrove's company. Next came the 40 in Capt. Walter Wilson's, Capt. John Norris's, and at the camp's southwestern corner, the 55 in Capt. Jacob Warrick's.

Riflemen on the camp's short sides guarded the flanks of the two lines. On the 150-yard-long left flank, Wells commanded about 165 in three companies. On the left, next to Barton's company, was his two-company Mounted Rifle battalion, which contained Geiger's 60 Kentucky horsemen and Robb's 60 from Indiana. Beyond, next to Hawkins' company, was Capt. James Bigger's 45-man company of Indiana riflemen on foot. On the 80-yard right flank, between Scott's and Warrick's companies, were the 85 Indiana men in Capt. Spier Spencer's oversize mounted rifle company, known as the "Yellow Jackets."

Within the camp, in the area behind Bigger's, Hawkins' and Larrabee's company, was the army's reserve, the 130 dragoons in Daviess's three-troop squadron. Capt. Benjamin Parke's 75 Indiana horsemen were posted behind Hawkins' company, and behind them, Capt. Charles Beggs' 30 more. To Beggs' right were the 25 Kentuckians that Funk had brought from Louisville. To their southwest were the tents of Harrison and the other senior officers, the army's parked wagons, piles of unpacked stores, horses, and 40 remaining cattle.

This photograph, taken at the 2011 bicentennial re-enactment of the battle, shows the general appearance of Harrison's 16th Camp. (Photograph by Dan Hester)

Around the camp, the Americans built an oval of fires, located about 10–15 yards ahead of their tents, lean-tos, and assigned sleeping locations. As the sunlight faded, the fires cooked suppers and warmed tired men. The talk around them was of whether the Indians would attack. Some were unconcerned. "Having seen a number of squaws and children at the town," recalled Sgt. Isaac Naylor of Bigger's company, "I thought the Indians were not disposed to fight." But the noise from distant Prophetstown was ominous. "Sam," an Indiana militiaman remembered his father saying, "sleep with your moccasins on. Them red devils are going to fight before day."

As the tired Americans ate their suppers, their commander gave new orders to his senior officers. An hour before sunrise, three taps on a drum, repeated in sequence, would direct the captains to form their companies in battle lines. The army also would be prepared for a surprise attack that night. All men were to sleep with their firearms, with muskets loaded and bayonets attached. All were to wear their cartridge boxes. "The position of the men during the night," recalled Cook, "together with myself, whilst at rest was lying on our arms with our clothes on. As for myself, I lay with my boots on, greatcoat on, and accoutrements buckled around me, with my rifle in my arms."

The ground ahead of the American perimeter varied in terrain. Ahead of the front line, a grove of a trees about 30 yards wide diminished in density and width as it led to the right. Beyond, the ground sloped down about 20 feet to marsh and prairie. On the rear line, Barton's men faced about 50 yards of woods, beyond which Burnett Creek flowed toward the camp below a cliff. Cook's and Peters' men were atop the cliff, and those in the other rear-line companies, above a gentler rise, faced the branches of oaks and willows rising from about 25 feet below. The men on the left flank could see only trees on the hundreds of yards of high ground beyond them. Those on the right faced about a hundred yards of woods before the ridge descended into marshland.

Bartholomew, the field officer of the day, would command the camp guards, who would be stationed about 75 yards beyond the camp perimeter. The guard consisted of Peters, Bigger, two other officers, and 132 men. Half would be posted as sentinels about 25 yards apart, watching in five-hour shifts beginning at 6.00pm. The others would remain at four guard outposts. In case of attack, they were to delay the Indians as long as possible while the men in the camp formed their companies.

As night approached, the guards chosen for the first shift of sentinel duty hurried to their positions to inspect the ground in the fading light. Private William Brigham of Hawkins' company, assigned a location on Burnett Creek, "took post a little after sunset. William Brown (a regular) was the sentinel on my left, and a militia man on my right. These three posts were directly in front of Capt. Barton's company of US Infantry." "I examined

Spencer's "Yellow Jackets" derived their name from their uniforms, hunting frocks with the fringe dyed yellow. These re-enactors in Corydon, Indiana, show their appearance. (Graphic Enterprises)

the ground adjacent to my post very particularly," he remembered. "There was a small thicket of willows, on a stream of water, about two rods in front of my post, and high grass between me and the willows. I observed it to be a favorable place for the approach of Indians and determined to be on the alert."

When the last sunlight left the sky at 6.08pm, the American fires continued to burn in the cold rain. Many of the men left their assigned sleeping positions for warmer sites. Naylor and his friend Pvt. Joseph Warnock were among those who found a fire ahead of Bigger's company. "Warnock and myself retired to rest," Naylor remembered, "he taking one side of the fire and I the other, the other members of our company being all asleep… Warnock had dreamed the night before a bad dream which foreboded something fatal to him or to some of his family, as he told me. Having myself no confidence in dreams, I thought but little about the matter, although I observed that he never smiled afterwards."

Ahead of the camp, Peters, Bigger, and the other guard officers huddled around their guard outpost fires. Each, accompanied by four noncommissioned officers, toured the sentinels' positions at intervals, responding to their challenges with the night's watchword, "All's well." "The night," Peters remembered, "was one of the darkest I ever saw. The wind blew. It was so cold and the rain poured down in torrents."

The sentinels were not entirely luckless. They at least had been given greatcoats to protect them. But their duty was terrifying. "It was," Brigham recalled "so very dark that no object could be discerned within three feet of me, and I could hear nothing except the rustling noise occasioned by the falling rain among the bushes."

The photograph shows the central feature of the standard carried by the 4th US Infantry Regiment at Tippecanoe, a gathering of eagles bearing arms. Captured by the British 41st Regiment of Foot when Governor William Hull surrendered Detroit without resistance in 1812, it now is displayed at the unit's regimental museum. (From the collections of the Regimental Museum of the Royal Welsh (Brecon), displayed at Firing Line, Cardiff Castle Museum of the Welsh Soldier)

At 11.00pm, when a relieved Brigham ended his shift, the Indians at Prophetstown had been waiting for hours for Tenskwatawa to announce that a vision had revealed victory in an attack. Finally word came. Harrison must die, Tenskatawa said. In the morning, he proposed, he would meet with the American commander, agree to abandon Prophetstown, and leave. Two warriors would linger after his departure and kill Harrison. The American commander's death, he had seen, would leave the Americans unable to fight. A massacre would follow, and then a bounty of captives and horses.

The announcement failed to satisfy the warriors. The Winnebagos, Tenskwatawa later would complain, had been the worst. Eager for battle, they could not be persuaded to wait until the following morning. When they demanded another vision, the shaman retired to seek further guidance.

When Tenskwatawa returned, he announced that the American commander could be killed that night. As other Indians surrounded the camp, warriors could infiltrate it and kill him. After Harrison's death, the shaman had seen, the Indians would fight in darkness against Americans revealed to them by light. And the Americans' weapons, he added, would be powerless to harm them.

Tenskwatawa left the task of planning and leading the operation to chiefs with reputations as military leaders. The Indians, they agreed, would attack the American camp in the usual way. The horns of an advancing Indian crescent would meet behind the camp to complete its encirclement. Mengoatowa's Kickapoos would form the right horn and Waweapakoosa's Winnebagos the left. Wabaunsee's Potawatomis, and the other Indians, led by Roundhead, would form the base. When the Kickapoos reached the most vulnerable area of the camp's perimeter, at its northeastern corner, a party of warriors would infiltrate the camp. When they signaled that Harrison was dead, the surrounding Indians would attack.

It would be a massacre like Wabash, the confident Indians thought. The anniversary of the greatest of Indian victories over the Americans had been three days before. The date, Harrison had written to Eustis after crossing the Wabash River, "has been marked in our calendar for the last 20 years." And like St Clair on November 4, 1791, the American commander now had compressed his encamped army onto a small area of high ground.

But if Harrison's assassination did not leave the Americans helpless, there were differences between this field and Wabash that might prove important. Except along the American right and left flanks, there were no woods like those that had protected the Indians at Wabash. There they had had 1,400 warriors to surround 1,700 Americans; here they had only about 500 to encircle 1,000. And there, they had not fought at night. Here, the Indian commanders would have to use whistles and rattles made from dried deer hooves to communicate their orders.

The appearance today of Prophet's Rock. (Author's photograph)

4.00–5.45am

When Brigham returned to his sentinel post at 4.00am, the first daylight was still three hours away. Tenskwatawa, his wife, and several chiefs left Prophetstown for high ground beyond Burnett Creek where they would watch the battle. From the site, which would be remembered as Prophet's Rock, they could see, about 400 yards to the east, the fires that marked the location of the American camp.

As Harrison's men slept or huddled by the fires, the Indian commanders led their warriors across the prairie. Impatient to begin their infiltration of the American camp, the Kickapoos reached the sentinels ahead of Barton's and Geiger's companies and began crawling silently forward between them. The remainder of the Indian crescent trailed behind them in the darkness in a rough, broken line. At its end were the Winnebagos, who had begun moving forward through the prairie far to the southeast.

THE AMERICAN LEFT FLANK, NOVEMBER 7, 1811, 5.50AM (PP. 64–65)

After being detected by American sentinels posted in the woods in the background, about 125 Kickapoos have attacked the American camp. They now have reached its northwestern corner, which is occupied by Capt. Robert Barton's 4th US Infantry Regiment company and Capt. Frederick Geiger's mounted rifle company of Kentucky Volunteers. The scene shows the fighting in Geiger's area. This man from Geiger's company **(1)**, wearing a blanket coat, and another **(2)**, kneeling to his right, have fired their rifles. This American **(3)**, fleeing from the Kickapoos, is wearing the watchcoat of an American sentinel. The green uniform beneath his coat shows that he is from Lt. Abraham Hawkins' US Rifle Regiment company. One of the camp guards who has fled from the woods, Daniel Pettit of Capt. James Bigger's Indiana Territory militia company, **(4)** is running with his bandana burning, set afire by the firing of an Indian musket at close range. This Kentuckian **(5)** is racing with a knife to cut his way into Geiger's tent, where Geiger **(6)** and a Kickapoo **(7)**, are fighting. This soldier from Barton's company **(8)** has fled from the Indian attack in his company's area, to the left of the scene, only to find that they are attacking Geiger's area too. A Kickapoo **(9)** has halted to scalp a dead Kentuckian. More Kickapoos **(10)** are running through the woods to join the attack.

By 5.00am, Larrabee remembered, "Some of the troops were up, and sitting by the fires; many of which had been furnished with fresh fuel, and the light arising from them, must have afforded the Indians a pretty correct view of our situation, and of the most proper place to make their assault." Naylor was among those who had risen. "I awoke" he recalled, "after a sound and refreshing sleep, having heard in a dream the firing of guns and the whistling of bullets just before I awoke from my slumber. A drizzling rain was falling and all things were still and quiet throughout the camp."

The appearance today of the area where the Kickapoos crept through the American sentinels, as seen from the right flank of Barton's company. (Photograph by Jonathan Winkler)

At 5.30am, Harrison awoke, and summoned his aides, his horse, and a drummer. A few minutes later, Sgt. Montgomery Orr of Barton's company awoke in the tent he shared with Corp. Daniel Thompson. He was, he remembered, "partly asleep, when some person rushed by and touched the corner of the tent. I sprang partly up."

By 5.45am, Harrison was about to order his drummer to awaken his men. Orr, who had gone back to sleep, was disturbed again. "Something," he told Thompson, "struck the top of the tent." Thompson, he remembered, then "rose up and took his gun."

Beyond the camp perimeter, Pvt. William Brown of Hawkins' company left his post and went to talk to Brigham, the sentinel to his right. "I heard light footsteps," Brigham remembered, "presented my gun, and should have fired upon him had he not that moment spoke, much agitated. 'Brigham, let us fire and run in. You may depend on it there are Indians in the bushes.' I told him not to fire yet for fear we should give a false alarm. While we were standing together, something struck in the brush near us, (I suppose an arrow). We were both frightened and run in without firing."

Corporal Stephen Mars of Geiger's company, a sentinel to Brigham's right, then fired on something he glimpsed in the dark. Naylor was sitting by a fire, "engaged," he remembered, "in making a calculation when I should arrive at home. I heard the crack of a rifle I had just time to think that some sentinel was alarmed and had fired his rifle without a real cause, when I heard the crack of another rifle, followed by an awful Indian yell all around the encampment."

Then there were shots within the camp. "Three or four rifles," Orr recalled, "were discharged at the very door of the tent." Thompson looked out, and then fell back. Orr shouted at him. But his friend, Orr remembered, "made me no answer, for he was a dead man. I got out of the tent as soon as possible. The men were in confusion, some in front and some in the rear of the tents firing, the Indians within a rod of us."

Ahead of Geiger's company, the guards and sentinels fled back to the camp. Daniel Pettit of Bigger's company, Naylor recalled, "was pursued so closely and furiously by an Indian as he was running from the guard fire to our lines, that to save his life he cocked his rifle as he ran and turning suddenly round, placed the muzzle of his gun against the body of the Indian and shot an ounce ball through him. The Indian fired his gun at the same

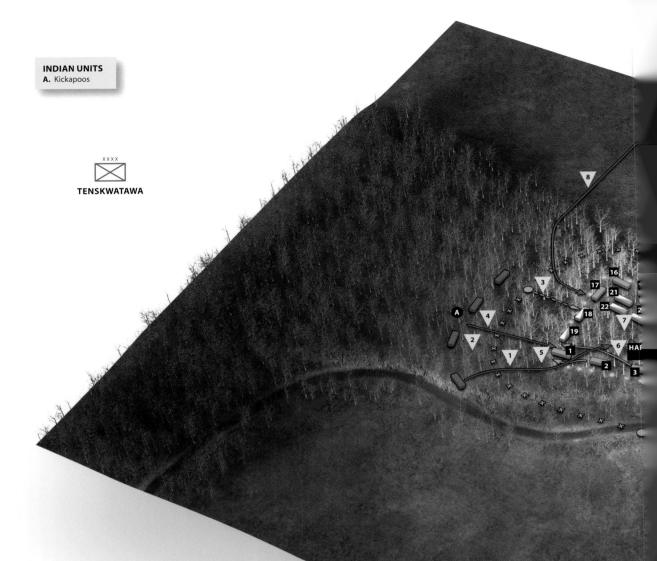

INDIAN UNITS
A. Kickapoos

XXXX
TENSKWATAWA

8

3

16

17

21

A

4

18

22

2

7

19

2

1

6

HAR

1

5

2

3

▼ **EVENTS**

1. As the Kickapoos move to encircle the camp from the north, some infiltrate the northwestern corner of the American camp, intending to kill Harrison.

2. Corporal Stephen Mars detects and kills an infiltrator, beginning the battle.

3. American guards and sentinels flee to the American camp.

4. Kickapoos attack Barton's and Geiger's companies.

5. Cook's company drives the Kickapoos from the area of Barton's company.

6. Peters' company drives the Kickapoos from the area of Geiger's company.

7. Indians who had reached the center of the American camp are hunted down and killed.

8. Arriving Potawatomis begin attacking Robb's and Bigger's companies.

9. Arriving Shawnees, Wyandots, and other Indians, after encountering cattle and horses fleeing from the American camp, begin attacking the American front line.

10. Arriving Winnebagos begin attacking the American right flank.

11. Harrison orders the American campfires extinguished.

THE INDIAN ATTACK: NOVEMBER 7, 1811, 5.45–6.00AM

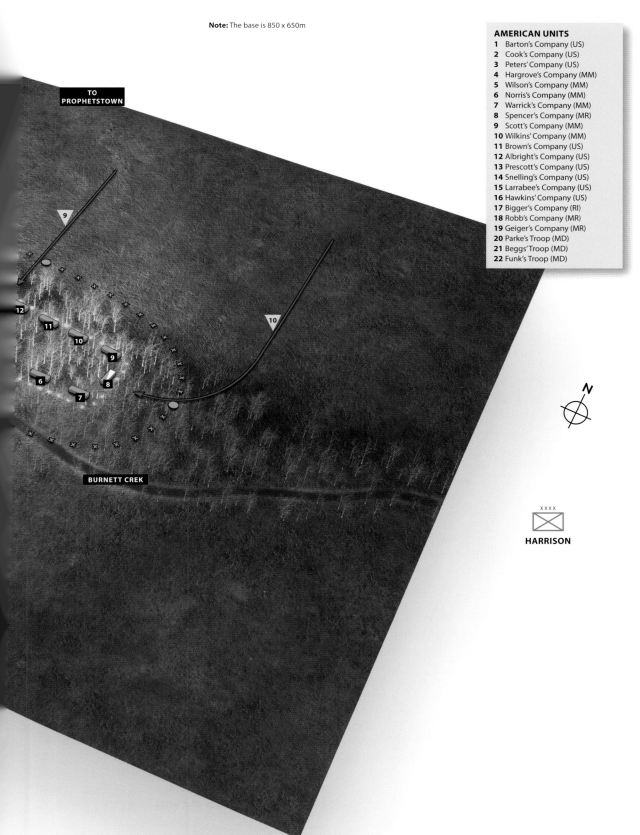

Note: The base is 850 x 650m

TO
PROPHETSTOWN

BURNETT CREK

HARRISON

"A bloody combat," Tipton wrote in his journal, "took place at precisely 15 minutes before 5 in the morning, which lasted two hours and 20 minutes." Tipton's watch recorded the time an hour earlier than Eastern Standard Time, which now is used in the area. This early 19th-century timepiece, displayed at the Champaign County (Ohio) Historical Society, belonged to the frontiersman Simon Kenton. (Photograph by James L. Graham)

instant, but it being longer than Pettit's muzzle passed by him and set fire to a handkerchief which he had tied around his head."

"Within a minute," Naylor remembered, the Indians reached the area where Geiger's men were camped. "I saw," he recalled, "the Indians charging our line most furiously and shooting a great many rifle balls into our camp fires, throwing the live coals into the air three or four feet high. At this moment my friend Warnock was shot by a rifle ball through his body. He ran a few yards and fell dead on the ground."

Hearing the firing, the Indians advancing in the prairie began moving more quickly toward the American fires. Ahead of the front line, Peters recalled, "a gun was fired by one of my sentries on which the Indians immediately rose up and fired on my guard as they were forming. Killed two and wounded several and giving their war yells rushed forward with dreadful fury. My guard ran (in spite of my exertions to detain them), some even leaving their arms behind."

Left without guards to command, Peters nonetheless tried to obey Harrison's orders. "Thus finding myself alone," he recalled, "I seized a rifle and, slipping behind a tree, waited the approach of the terrible enemy. I had scarcely taken up my post when an Indian flashed his piece at me within the distance of a rod, his rifle missing fire perhaps saved my life. I then thought it time to discharge my rifle at my antagonist and make tracks for my own safety."

On the American right flank, the Yellow Jackets could hear the shots and screams from 300 yards to the north. There Tipton looked at his pocket watch. "This is it," he thought. And he wanted to remember exactly when it began.

5.45–6.00am

At the northwestern corner of the camp, there was chaos. Baen, who rushed to the area to form a defensive line, was tomahawked. "Captain Barton," Orr remembered, "ordered the men to form instantly. They were too much broken, and no regular line could be formed, but they kept up a steady fire on the Indians, who fell back." Barton's men, Walker recalled, "sprang from their tents and discharged their pieces upon the enemy, with great execution."

It was worse to their right. "Capt. Geiger's company of militia, stationed near us," Orr remembered, "were in great confusion. They could hardly be distinguished from the Indians." "One Indian," Naylor recalled, "was killed in the back part of Captain Geiger's tent, while he was attempting to tomahawk the captain."

Alarmed by the gunfire, the American cattle and untethered horses began rushing down into the marsh and prairie. As they stampeded into the darkness, Harrison mounted a bay instead of his usual light gray horse. He and Owen, who was mounted on a white horse, immediately rode toward the left flank. Fearing for their commander's safety, some of the dragoon officers tried to persuade Harrison not to enter the area. Lieutenant Thomas

Emerson of Parke's troop seized his bridle, but Harrison spurred his horse on. When an Indian ball then killed Owen, word that the American commander had fallen spread through the Indian ranks.

Harrison was furious at the failure of his left flank guards to give the American units in the camp time to form for battle. The guards, he later wrote, "made not the least resistance, but abandoned their officer and fled into camp." But Barton's and Geiger's men, he remembered, "even under these circumstances seized their arms and took their stations."

And elsewhere, the Americans immediately assumed their battle positions. On the front line, remembered Larrabee, "A few seconds passed before the line of battle was formed, after which, the Indians found the army ready to meet them on all points." On the rear line, many of the soldiers were in formation even before their officers reached them. "At the report of the gun," wrote Cook, "I had no more to do than throw off my blanket, put my hat on and go to my company, which was eight or ten steps from my tent."

The dragoons also were ready. "I immediately mounted my troop," Funk remembered, "which had been stationed near Gov. Harrison's marquee. Finding that the enemy's missiles reached some of my men while they were unable to annoy their foe, Harrison ordered us to dismount and, with saber and pistol in hand, to stand beside our horses, ready to repel any attack that should force the lines of infantry in front."

Harrison sent two companies of regulars to the northeastern corner of the camp to drive the Indians back. With bayonets fixed, Cook's company, which adjoined Barton's, wheeled to its right and charged. Peters, who had just returned to his company, led his men around Cook's right. To their commander's relief, they effected the maneuver smoothly in the darkness. His men, Peters remembered, "wheeled instantly and marched up to support the

This 1840 Nathaniel Currier lithograph shows Lt. Thomas Emerson trying to stop Harrison from riding into the area where Barton's and Geiger's companies were under attack. (Library of Congress, Prints and Photographs Division)

retreating militia… We passed the confused retreat and met the Indians and charged them outside of the camp." As the Indians fell back, Hargrove's men spread out to the north to occupy the positions left by the two charging companies.

But the American bayonets had not expelled all the Indians. Warriors had been seen far into the interior of the camp. Some had even reached the area of Funk's dragoons, near Harrison's headquarters tent. Eleven-year-old William Gaines, who had accompanied his uncle, Joseph Daviess, shared with one of Funk's sergeants a tent next to Daviess's. "We were surprised," he recalled, "by the Indians, who got in the camp before we were aware of it. Some rushed into our tent, but we crawled out on the opposite side. Before getting out, however, the thumb of my left hand was cut by an Indian tomahawk or knife and laid wide open."

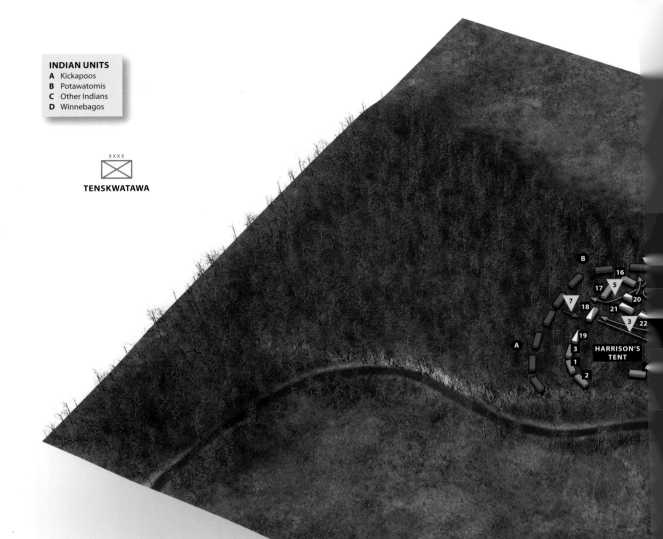

INDIAN UNITS
A Kickapoos
B Potawatomis
C Other Indians
D Winnebagos

xxxx

TENSKWATAWA

**HARRISON'S
TENT**

▼ EVENTS

1. Daviess and 20 dismounted dragoons attempt to dislodge the Potawatomis from woods ahead of Hawkins' company.

2. Snelling's company expels the Potawatomis from woods.

3. Robb's company collapses and flees to the center of the camp.

4. Prescott's company occupies the area left by Robb's company.

5. Snelling's company drives the Indians from the woods ahead of Bigger's company.

6. Dismounted dragoons occupy the area of the front line previously held by Snelling's and Prescott's companies.

7. Kickapoos and Potawatomis repeatedly attack the American left flank.

8. Additional Winnebagos reach the American right flank.

9. Winnebagos attack Spencer's and Warrick's companies.

10. Robb's company reinforces Spencer's and Warrick's companies.

11. Larrabee's company reinforces Spencer's and Robb's companies.

12. Larrabee's, Spencer's and Robb's companies drive the Winnebagos back.

THE AMERICAN DEFENSE: NOVEMBER 7, 1811, 6.00AM–7.15AM

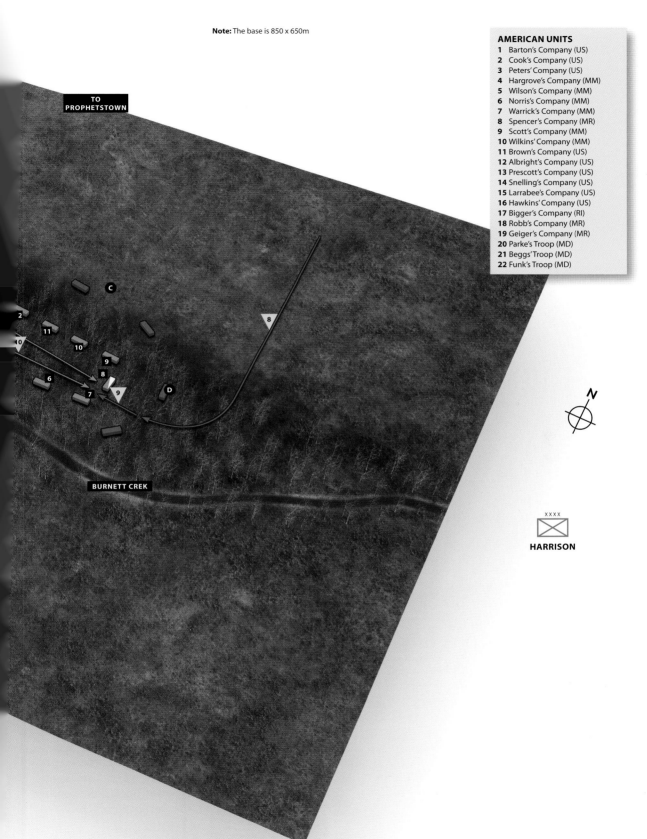

Note: The base is 850 x 650m

TO PROPHETSTOWN

BURNETT CREK

AMERICAN UNITS
1 Barton's Company (US)
2 Cook's Company (US)
3 Peters' Company (US)
4 Hargrove's Company (MM)
5 Wilson's Company (MM)
6 Norris's Company (MM)
7 Warrick's Company (MM)
8 Spencer's Company (MR)
9 Scott's Company (MM)
10 Wilkins' Company (MM)
11 Brown's Company (US)
12 Albright's Company (US)
13 Prescott's Company (US)
14 Snelling's Company (US)
15 Larrabee's Company (US)
16 Hawkins' Company (US)
17 Bigger's Company (RI)
18 Robb's Company (MR)
19 Geiger's Company (MR)
20 Parke's Troop (MD)
21 Beggs' Troop (MD)
22 Funk's Troop (MD)

N

HARRISON

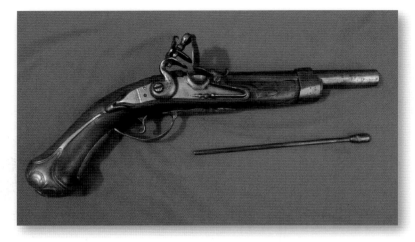

An American officer carried this pistol at the battle. (Grouseland Foundation, Vincennes, Indiana)

A frantic search for the hiding invaders now began. Men with torches and pistols looked behind trees, under wagons, and in tents. One by one, the warriors were found. "In a few moments," Naylor remembered, "they were all killed."

Harrison paced his horse around the American perimeter, inspecting conditions in every area. With every tour, he saw the arc of Indian fire grow greater. Soon it "extended along the left flank, the whole of the front, the right flank, and part of the rear." The horrified American commander then realized what he had failed to foresee.

Sergeant Richard Fillebrown of Snelling's company had been the first American to recognize the problem. When Snelling heard the Indians' shots and screams, the 30-year-old captain recalled, "I seized my sword and ran to the door of my tent where I met the orderly sergeant of my company, who asked me if the company should form in front or rear of the tents. The men were then in the rear and, recollecting that the light of the fires in front would expose them to the fire of the enemy and probably occasion some confusion, I directed them to form in the rear and countermarch to the front."

But in battle lines 5–10 yards behind their fires, Harrison realized, the Americans would be like actors on a stage in a darkened theater, illuminated by footlights for an audience they could not see. He instantly ordered the fires put out. "The large fires were immediately extinguished," Larrabee recalled, "for they afforded the enemy a great chance in viewing the camp."

Soon darkness spread along the front and rear lines, and on the American right flank. But at the northeastern corner of the camp, men fell as they approached the blazes. The work, Walker recalled, "could not be but imperfectly accomplished, as the Indian marksmen were sure to pick off whoever approached them."

These reproduction cartridges are displayed at the Tippecanoe Battlefield Museum. The opened cartridge shows the load prescribed by Anthony Wayne for US Army infantrymen in 1793: powder, a ball, and three buckshot. (Author's photograph)

As the glow from the American camp began to diminish, Tenskwatawa chanted atop Prophet's Rock, summoning the power of the Great Spirit to aid the Indians. But Harrison had not been killed. And the detection of the infiltrating Kickapoos had left the Indian commanders' battle plan in ruins.

The engagement had begun before the Indian crescent had encircled the American camp. In the north, the Kickapoos on the far Indian right had fallen back from Cook's and Peters' charge. To their left, arriving Potawatomis were attacking Robb's and Bigger's positions. In the south, Winnebagos at the far Indian left were beginning to find battle positions opposite Warrick's and Spencer's men. Between the Potawatomis and Winnebagos, where the American cattle and horses had stampeded, a few Indians were firing on the American front line. More were moving forward through the rain toward the sound of gunfire. But many others, eager to get horses, were moving away to search in the prairie for those that had fled from the American camp.

6.00–6.30am

Except near the dwindling fires at the northeastern corner of the camp, the battle now was fought in darkness. "Nothing," remembered Funk, "could be seen but the flashes of the enemy's guns." The American commander was in ceaseless motion, invisible but heard as he circled around the American perimeter. "The clear, calm voice of General Harrison," Naylor recalled, "was heard in words of heroism in every part of the encampment during the action." "His voice," Walker remembered, " was frequently heard and easily distinguished, giving his orders in the same calm, cool, and collected manner with which we had been used to receive them on a drill or parade."

This Matthew Harris Jouett portrait, painted about 1810, depicts Joseph H. Daviess. Although usually referred to by that name, his surname actually was spelled Daveiss. (Filson Historical Society, Louisville, Kentucky)

Everywhere, the American commander noted with satisfaction, his musketry was standing firm. Against Indians who instantly found new positions after firing, the weapons of the American riflemen were useless at night. But the Americans with muskets had found themselves ideally armed to respond to such fire.

At Fallen Timbers, Wayne had issued to a special body of light infantrymen cartridges containing buckshot rather than balls. Harrison had provided similar munitions for all of his muskets. When an American with a musket saw the flash of exploding Indian powder, he could send towards it like bees from a disturbed hive an expanding disk of 12 buckshot, which at 50 yards was about 4 feet in diameter, and at 100 about 8 feet. "We were well supplied with buck shot cartridges," Walker remembered, "which were admirably calculated for an engagement of this nature... The savages were severely galled by the steady and well directed fire of the troops."

As more Potawatomis arrived, the pressure grew on Hawkins' and Larrabee's companies at the left of the American front line. "These two companies." Larrabee recalled, "not only had to contend with the enemy in front, but those at the head of the camp that were nigh this angle."

Protected by woods, the Potawatomis ahead of Hawkins' company pushed forward until they were behind trees only 10 yards from the Americans. "The small company of US riflemen, commanded by Lieut. Hawkins," remembered Walker, "were stationed within two rods of these trees, and received the heaviest of their fire, but maintained the position in a most gallant manner."

THE AMERICAN RIGHT FLANK, NOVEMBER 7, 1811, 7.00AM (PP. 76–77)

Winnebago Indians attacked the southwestern corner of the American camp, occupied by Capts. Spier Spencer's and Jacob Warrick's Indiana Territory militia companies. In confused fighting in the dark, Spencer, Warrick, and most of the companies' other officers were killed. Captain David Robb's militia company then stiffened the American resistance. Now, after the first sunlight of a new day has begun to illuminate the field, Lt. Charles Larrabee's 4th US Infantry Regiment company has arrived. The men at the head of Larrabee's 40-man column **(1)** are waiting in single file for orders. Their sergeant **(2)** is listening as Robb **(3)**, whose men are scattered among Spencer's, explains that they are going to form a line to charge the Indians, with his men to the right of the regulars, and Spencer's to the left. A fallen militiaman **(4)** lies

ahead. The yellow fringe on his hunting frock shows that he was in Spencer's company, known as the Yellow Jackets. A militiaman from Robb's company **(5)**, dressed in a blanket coat, is firing his rifle, as another **(6)**, from Spencer's, reloads. Larrabee **(7)**, who has taken command in the area, is talking with Ens. John Tipton **(8)**, who now leads the Yellow Jackets, and Capt. John Smith **(9)**, whose small unit had been incorporated into Warrick's. Smith, who has assumed command of Warrick's company, is reporting that his men have halted the Indian advance on their front, beyond the scene to the right. In the distance, two Winnebagos **(10)** have fired on the Americans, as others **(11)** move to new firing positions.

Daviess, whose dragoons were posted behind Hawkins and Larrabee, was impatient for action. The great lawyer, Harrison remembered 25 years later, "insisted on having something to do, disliking very much to stand holding horses while the infantry were so hard pressed." When Daviess repeatedly asked for permission to use his dismounted dragoons to dislodge the Indians from the trees, the American commander finally assented.

Dressed in a white blanket coat, the dragoon commander quickly found 20 men armed with sabers and pistols. After forming them into a column, he led them into the trees. "The major's undaunted courage," Larrabee judged, "hurried him forward with too small a force to assure success." "He was easily distinguished by the Indians," Walker remembered, "and received three balls in his body. "I am a dead man," the Kentuckian cried as he fell. When the Indians killed Isaac White and wounded another man, the dragoons retreated.

The American commander then sent Snelling's company to drive the Indians from the troublesome woods with buckshot and bayonets. "The Indians," Harrison reported to Eustis, were "immediately and gallantly dislodged from their advantageous position." The warriors, Larrabee remembered with satisfaction, "found too warm a reception and left the ground in front."

But to the left, the Kickapoos and Potawatomis were pushing Robb's and Bigger's men back. Unable to find targets for their balls, the Indiana Territory riflemen had begun retiring, seeking safety in a greater distance from the invisible, scalp-seeking wraiths ahead. Bigger stopped his men's retreat, but the retirement of the Knox County riflemen became a flight. Robb's men, remembered Walker, "fell back in great disorder." Their conduct, fumed a furious Boyd, was "dastardly."

When Harrison learned of the collapse of Robb's unit, he sent Prescott's company from the center of the front line to the area the Indiana Territory riflemen had abandoned. He then sent Snelling's company for a second charge, this time to drive back the Indians threatening Bigger's riflemen. The dismounted dragoons, now led by Parke, were ordered to occupy the area of the front line left by Snelling's and Prescott's companies. "Capts. Snelling and Prescott," Larrabee remembered, "was ordered from this wing, to support the line across the head of the camp, their vacancy supplied with dragoons. Capt. Snelling charged and dislodged a body of Indians in that direction and nigh this angle."

Daviess and White died carrying each other's swords, which their families later exchanged. The photograph shows White's hat and sword. (Courtesy of the White County, Indiana, Historical Society)

6.30–7.15am

About 6.30am, when the first daylight was less than half an hour away, Tenskwatawa left his rock and began moving back to Prophetstown. Along the American left flank, front line, and right flank, the Indians continued their assaults. "The manner the Indians fought," recalled Larrabee, "was desperate. They would rush with

THE AMERICAN COUNTERATTACK, NOVEMBER 7, 1811, 7.40AM (PP. 80–81)

The Americans have charged with bayonets the Kickapoos and Potawatomis in the woods ahead of the American left flank. The scene is the left wing of the charge. A Kickapoo who has exhausted his powder (1) has dropped his musket and is preparing to battle the advancing Americans with a spear. This Kickapoo (2) has fired his musket as yet another (3) is reloading his. The Indian commander Mengoatowa (4), leaning against a tree, is covering with leaves a wound that will prove fatal. Although a Kickapoo, he is dressed in the uniform and paint worn by chiefs of different tribes on Tecumseh's visit to the southern Indians. He has asked his brother (5) to retrieve from the ground his war club. The Potawatomi commander Wabaunsee (6), whose people are fighting to the left of the Kickapoos, is telling Mengoatowa that the Potawatomis are retreating toward Prophetstown. Other Kickapoos (7) are fleeing from the approaching American bayonets. In the distance, Capt. Thomas Scott's Knox County company of Indiana Territory militiamen (8) is advancing while a dragoon from Capt. Peter Funk's troop (9) is charging through a gap in the American line. Beyond him, Capt. George Prescott's 4th US Infantry Regiment company (10) and Capt. Walter Wilson's Knox County militiamen (11) are advancing. Beyond Wilson's company, visible in the far distance, are riflemen from Capt. Frederick Geiger's Kentucky company (12), who are leaving, at intervals, men to guard the charge's left flank from Indian attack.

horrid yells in bodies upon the lines. Being driven back, they would remain in perfect silence for a few seconds, then would whistle (on an instrument made for that purpose) and then commence the rush again, while others would creep up close to the lines on their hands and knees, and get behind trees for their support."

Again and again, the Indians attacked the Americans on the left flank and left of the front line. In the area defended by Barton's, Peters', and Geiger's companies and his own, Cook recalled, it took another bayonet charge before the warriors at last retired to a respectful distance. Where Prescott's, Snelling's, and Bigger's companies defended the perimeter, Naylor remembered, the Indians "made four or five most fierce charges on our lines, yelling and screaming as they advanced, shooting balls and arrows into our ranks. At each charge they were driven back in confusion, carrying off their dead and wounded as they retreated."

The Winnebagos, who had been the last to reach the field, finally assembled all their units on the American right flank. Now they would try to break through the Ameri- can perimeter while darkness remained. From the trees along Burnett Creek and at the low end of the ridge, they moved forward against the southwestern corner of the American camp.

After climbing to the high ground on the ridge, they attacked Spencer's Yellow Jackets and the left flank of Warrick's rear line company. A ball hit Spencer in the head. Two more hit his legs. A final ball in his chest proved fatal. Then Warrick fell mortally wounded.

Upon learning of this new assault, Harrison rode quickly to the south end of the camp. When he encountered a Yellow Jacket shouting orders in the chaos, he asked, "Where is the captain of this company?" "Dead, Sir." was the response. "The first lieutenant?" "The second lieutenant?" "Dead, Sir," were the replies again. "Where," the American commander finally asked, "is your ensign?" "Here, sir," responded Tipton, who 17 days before had been a private. "Stand fast," Harrison told him, "and I will get relief for you in a few minutes."

The minutes passed slowly. The buckshot and bayonets of Warrick's men, and Scott's on the front line, kept the Winnebagos from breaking through the areas to Tipton's right and left. But the hard-pressed Yellow Jackets, using their rifles as clubs, and wielding tomahawks and knives, could not distinguish friend from foe. His men, Tipton recalled, became "mixed among the Indians so that we could not tell the Indians and our men apart."

When the American commander returned to the center of the camp, he met Robb. The Knox County captain, who had reassembled his scattered men, was eager to redeem his company's reputation. Soon Robb's men were rushing to support Tipton's. Harrison also ordered Larrabee's company to move to the left flank.

Monuments now stand on the locations where the American commanders at Tippecanoe fell. These four, from Capt. Spier Spencer (left foreground) through his subordinates Lts. Richard McMahon and Thomas Berry, to Capt. Jacob Warrick (right background) trace the line upon which the men in Spencer's and Warrick's companies fought to hold the attacking Winnebagos back. (Photograph by Jonathan Winkler)

On November 7, 1836, the 25th anniversary of Tippecanoe, John Tipton would donate to the state of Indiana the land on which the battle had been fought. This engraving from M. W. Pershing's 1900 *Life of General John Tipton* depicts him in 1837. (Author's collection)

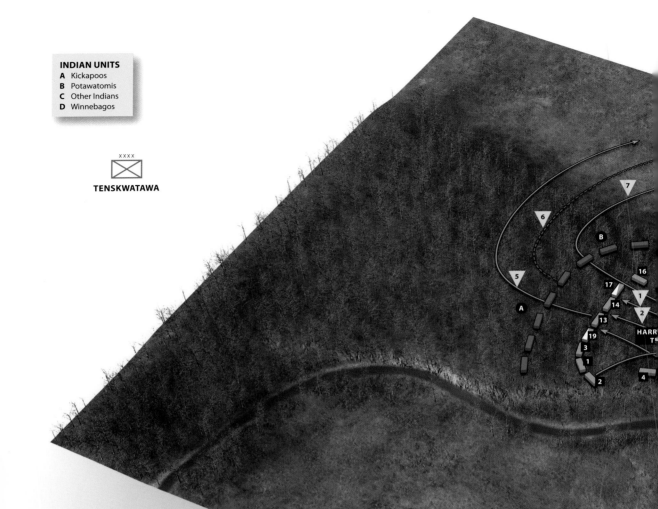

xxxx

TENSKWATAWA

EVENTS

1. Albright's company moves to the left flank.

2. Scott's company moves to the left flank.

3. Wilson's company moves to the left flank.

4. Cook's company moves to the right flank.

5. Led by Wells, Geiger's, Wilson's, Prescott's, Scott's, Snelling's, Albright's, and Bigger's companies charge and wheel to the right.

6. The Kickapoos and Potawatomis flee toward Prophetstown.

7. The dragoons with horses join the charge and pursue the Indians into the prairie.

8. Led by Cook, Spencer's, Cook's, Larrabee's, and Robb's companies charge and wheel to the left.

9. The Winnebagos flee toward Prophetstown.

10. The Indians facing the American front line flee toward Prophetstown.

THE AMERICAN COUNTERATTACK: NOVEMBER 7, 1811, 7.15–8.05 AM

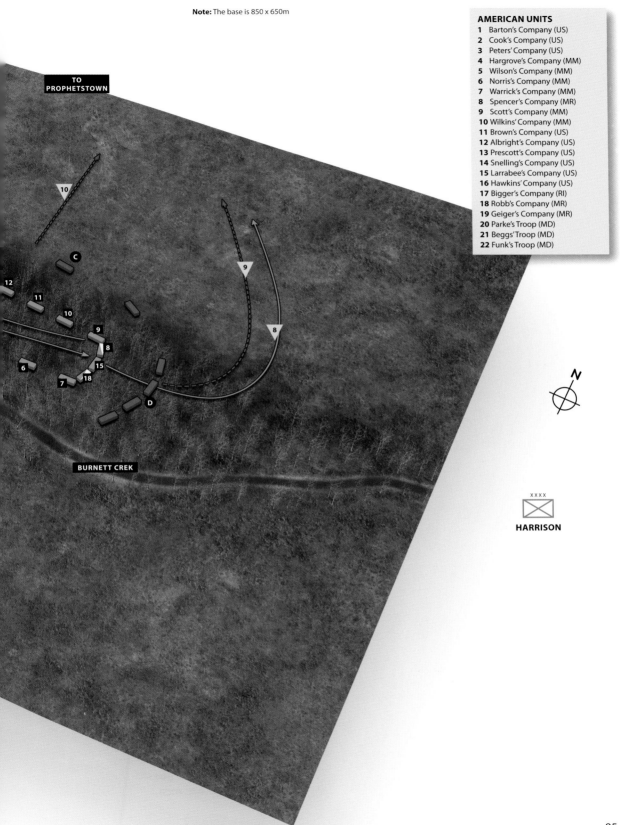

Note: The base is 850 x 650m

TO PROPHETSTOWN

BURNETT CREK

N

HARRISON

By 6.55am, when the first sunlight of a new day appeared, Larrabee had arrived at the scene. "The Indians," he remembered, "had gained ground upon Spencer's company." But Tipton's and Robb's riflemen, no longer blinded by the darkness, began to force the Winnebagos back. Larrabee then brought order to the chaos he had found. He "commanded and formed the companies," the 29-year-old lieutenant recalled, "charged the Indians, killed five and put the rest to flight."

7.15–8.05am

As the day grew brighter, the firing between the Indian and American lines continued. Like the other mounted officers, the now visible American commander attracted swarms of musket balls as he rode around the camp. One pierced his hat and creased his head, but Harrison rode on with a small stream of blood flowing down his face. He otherwise maintained the invulnerability to enemy fire that Tenskwatawa had promised the Indians.

Now the American commander could see the positions of the enemy. Concentrations faced the American flanks. A thin thread of warriors was opposite the American front line. A few scattered Indians were beyond the rear.

For an hour and a half, Harrison had fought a defensive battle. "My great object," he would report to Eustis, "was to keep the lines entire – to prevent the Indians from breaking into the camp, until daylight should enable me to make a general and effectual charge." Now the Americans would attack.

After sunrise, Harrison's men would charge with bayonets from both the right and left flanks. Wheeling toward the rising sun, they would drive the Indians from the woods into the grass ahead of the American front line. The dragoons then would pursue the fleeing warriors back to Prophetstown.

To assemble the forces that would attack, the American commander redeployed his units again. To the left flank, he sent Albright's and Scott's companies from the front line and Wilson's from the rear. To the right flank, he dispatched Cook's company from the left. And the dismounted dragoons on the front line, he ordered, now should find their horses.

When the sun appeared over the horizon at 7.24am, Wells, on the left flank, and Cook, on the right, were busy organizing the units that would charge. Funk's small dragoon troop was ready to mount. But many men from Parke's and Beggs' troops were searching the camp for horses.

Soon the men on the flanks were in their positions, awaiting, with bayonets poised, the order to charge. Minutes then passed as the dragoons' search for mounts continued. Wells, who had 300 men compressed into an area only 150 yards wide, grew increasingly unhappy at the delay. Twenty years before, the Kentuckian had seen at Wabash the consequences of exposing to continuous fire men who were too close together. Indian balls that missed their targets just hit other men.

The hat worn by Harrison at Tippecanoe. (Grouseland Foundation, Vincennes, Indiana)

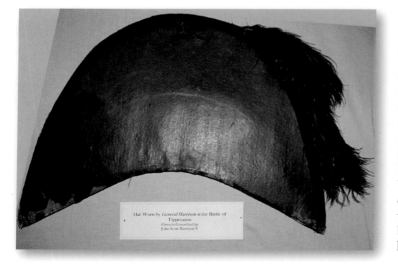

Hat Worn by *General Harrison* at the Battle of Tippecanoe
Given to Grouseland by
John Scott Harrison V

Finally Wells gave the order. Geiger's riflemen advanced obliquely to the left, and Bigger's to the right. The approximately 180 men in Wilson's, Prescott's, Scott's, Snelling's, and Albright's companies went forward in an ever-lengthening line. "Major Wells, who commanded on the left flank," Harrison reported to Eustis, "not knowing my intentions precisely… charged the enemy before I had formed the body of dragoons with which I meant to support the infantry."

As the overwhelmed Kickapoos and Potawatomis fell back, Harrison sent the dragoons with horses galloping north to join the charge. Then Cook ordered his men forward. Between Tipton's riflemen on the left, and Robb's on the right, the 80 bayonets of Cook's and Larrabee's men advanced against the Winnebagos. "We made a charge," Tipton recalled, "and drove them out of the timber across the prairie."

When fleeing Indians began to appear ahead of the American front line, Naylor recalled, "An almost deafening and universal shout was raised by our men. 'Huzza! Huzza! Huzza!'" "The Indians," Walker remembered, "fled in all directions, leaving us masters of the field, which was strewed with the bodies of the killed and wounded."

Harrison's pride in his little army was unbounded. The performance of his militiamen was especially gratifying. "Several of the militia companies," he wrote to Eustis, "were in no wise inferior to the regulars. Spencer's, Geiger's, and Warrick's companies maintained their posts amid a monstrous carnage, as, indeed, did Robb's after it was posted on the right flank." "The troops," he concluded, "nineteen-twentieths of whom had never been in action before, behaved in a manner that can never be too much applauded." "Our men," Tipton wrote in his journal after the battle, "fought brave."

But the cost of victory had been high. Among the officers, Baen, Daviess, Owen, Spencer, and Warrick had been killed, and Bartholomew, Decker, Geiger, Peters, and Norris wounded. His own survival, Harrison wrote to a close friend, he could attribute only to "providential interference." In all, the Americans had lost 62 dead and 126 wounded.

Harrison's men now were eager to attack Prophetstown. Their commander, however, was cautious. His men had killed, perhaps, 50 Indians and wounded another 100. But they had not destroyed the Prophet's army. And, a wounded Indian had said, hundreds of fresh warriors were rushing to reinforce it. The

The appearance today of the ground ahead of the American front line. (Photograph by Jonathan Winkler)

Americans, Harrison announced, would fortify the camp, and await another attack before advancing on Prophetstown.

As some of his soldiers began building 4-foot-high breastworks, and searching for the army's cattle and lost horses, others buried the dead and cared for the wounded. Walker was among those the surgeons treated. With him was a stricken Potawatomi chief. The Indian, Walker wrote in his journal on November 7, "expressed the greatest sorrow at what had happened and accused the Prophet of deceiving them."

FROM TIPPECANOE TO VINCENNES

When the sun set after the battle, Tipton recalled, "We lay all night at our breastwork without fire." At sunrise on November 8, Wells led a party of mounted riflemen toward Prophetstown. "They entered the town," Walker remembered, "and found an aged squaw only, who informed them that the Indians had left it in great haste immediately after the action."

Far to the south, Tecumseh had completed his tour of Creek villages. To the relief of William McIntosh and the other Creek chiefs, he announced after returning to Tuckabatchee that he and his party now would go to the villages of the Osages. The departing Shawnee left behind Seekaboo, who would continue his missionary work, and many Creeks like the young chief Ellipohorchem, who were eager to fight the Americans.

This colored lithograph from McKenney and Hall reproduced Charles Bird King's 1825 portrait of William McIntosh. (Author's collection)

Tecumseh left as well a prophecy. There would be a final sign, he said, that the Great Spirit had sent him. After he was gone, the Shawnee said in a last address in Tuckabatchee, he would "stamp his foot upon the ground and shake down every house in the town." He said, remembered the Creek George Stiggins, that he would "climb a mountain, whoop, clap his hands, and stamp on the earth 3 times until it trembled."

At Prophetstown, Harrison turned his attention to his army's almost exhausted food supply. As some men slaughtered the cattle that could be found, others butchered the horses that had fallen, Still others scoured Tenskwatawa's village for food. "I found large quantities of corn, beans and peas," remembered Naylor. "I filled my knapsack with these articles and carried them to the camp and divided them with the members of our mess, consisting of six men. Having these articles of food, we declined eating horse-flesh, which was eaten by a large portion of our men."

By 2.00pm on November 9, Prophetstown and its fields had been burned. With 18 wagons filled with wounded, and each soldier carrying what he would eat, the Americans left for home. After 8 miles, they halted at the army's 17th Camp, where Harrison took new precautions against a surprise attack at night. A circle of uniformed scarecrows guarded the camp, while the real sentinels watched from concealed positions. And the campfires were extinguished before the Americans went to sleep.

On November 10, Tipton wrote in his journal, "We moved early, traveling hard." Marching past its 15th Camp, the army halted after 15 miles at its 18th Camp. The following day, the food began to run out. Driven by their growing hunger, the Americans marched 25 miles to the site of their 13th Camp. "Lived today chiefly on parched corn," Tipton wrote.

On November 12, the weather turned worse. "We moved early through wet prairie," Tipton wrote. "All the water frozen over with ice which made it very bad for our foot men." But the starving, freezing, and slipping men knew what lay 18 miles ahead.

The door of Jonathan Alder's 1806 cabin, which is preserved at the Madison County (Ohio) Historical Society. (Author's photograph)

At last they reached Boyd's Blockhouse. From there the wounded could travel on water. And, a jubilant Tipton wrote, "Just as we arrived, the boat came up with provisions. We drawed beef, flour and whiskey."

The refreshed Americans soon marched to Fort Harrison, where they left Snelling's company to garrison the stronghold. By November 19, all had reached Vincennes. Indians professing friendship then began arriving in the Indiana Territory capitol.

They included the two most important Kickapoo chiefs. "These chiefs," Harrison wrote to Eustis, "say that the whole of the tribes who lost warriors in the late action attribute their misfortune to the Prophet alone; that they constantly reproach him with their misfortunes, and threaten him with death; that they are all desirous of making their peace with the United States."

News of the battle soon spread across the frontier. Alder was awakened early on November 10. "About 2 o'clock I heard a knock at the door," he remembered. "My Indian visitors told me that they had come to tell me that there had been a hard fight between the Indians and the whites on the Tippecanoe at Tecumseh's Town. The Indians made the attack in the night but were badly whipped." Now, Alder's visitors reported, he could "rest easy, for there would be no more fighting. They all said the thing was ended."

AFTERMATH

Thirty-six nights after the knock on his door, Alder was again disturbed at 2.00am. This time, the whole cabin shook. It was the first of what would be called the New Madrid Earthquakes. Four hundred miles to the west, Tecumseh and his party were camped near the epicenter, on their way to visit Osage villages.

But the Osages too had no interest in joining the Shawnee's union. As the weary Indians rode home, Tecumseh learned of the battle. And then, Tecumseh told Anthony Shane's father, the Wyandot chief Isadore Chesne, he saw at Prophetstown "the fruits of our labor destroyed, the bodies of my friends laying in the dust, our village burnt to the ground, and all our kettles carried off." His brother he found on nearby Wildcat Creek, camped with 40 Indians who had remained loyal. "Those I left at home," he told Chesne, "were – I cannot call them men – a poor set of people."

The time of the Prophet had passed. But Tecumseh was indomitable. He dispatched messengers to Main Poc and the other chiefs who favored war, and to trusted young warriors in Indian villages from the Great Lakes to the Gulf of Mexico. Prophetstown, the Shawnee announced, would be rebuilt. And the great war would begin "when the corn was high." Other messengers went to Fort Malden. The British, Tecumseh asked, should immediately send munitions to Prophetstown, where gunpowder was desperately needed. And he would himself come to Malden in early July.

The Shawnee also sent messengers to Vincennes. When the Indiana Territory governor learned of the rebuilding of Prophetstown, Tecumseh feared, he would march up the Wabash again. The Shawnee brothers, the messengers said, now wanted only peace. Tecumseh and Tenskwatawa would go to Washington to meet with President Madison.

Prophetstown soon began to rise again. Winnebagos built a village on Wildcat Creek, and Potawatomis another on the nearby Tippecanoe River. Ellipohorchem arrived with four warriors to report that, as Tecumseh had predicted, the ground had shaken at Tuckabatchee. Many Creeks now were ready to follow him to war.

As the Indiana Territory governor made arrangements for the Shawnee brothers' trip to Washington, Tecumseh nervously awaited a response from Fort Malden. Impatient young warriors daily increased the likelihood that the Americans would march against Prophetstown while the Indians were

The December 16, 1812 earthquake and the two that followed were the three most powerful known to have occurred in North America. The photograph shows the Mississippi River near New Madrid, Missouri. (Courtesy of the New Madrid Historical Museum)

incapable of effective resistance. On April 11, they massacred the Hutson family north of Vincennes, and on April 22 the Harrymans and their five children west of the town.

At last word arrived from the British. Twelve horse loads of munitions were waiting at Malden for the Indians to transport to Prophetstown. A confident Tecumseh then dispatched another messenger to Vincennes. He and his brother, he informed Harrison, would not go to Washington.

The furious Indiana Territory governor began to prepare for another campaign. But then disastrous news arrived. Expecting an imminent war with Britain, the American government had decided to send a large army to defend Detroit. On May 3, Harrison watched helplessly as Boyd's regiment left Vincennes to join it.

But war did not come as Tecumseh foresaw. While he was at Fort Malden, ready to lead the packhorse train back to Prophetstown, he learned that the United States had declared war on Britain on June 18. Offered command of the Indians who would fight as British allies, the Shawnee accepted.

At first, the memory of Tippecanoe dampened the enthusiasm of the Indians for a war with the Americans. But on August 16, Hull surrendered Detroit. Soon Forts Wayne and Harrison were besieged, and Harrison assumed command of American forces on the Northwest Frontier. In fierce fighting, the Americans again destroyed Prophetstown, repelled two British and Indian invasions of Ohio, and, at the September 10, 1813 battle of Lake Erie, seized control of the lake. Then the Americans, and Shawnees and Wyandots led by Black Hoof and Tarhe, invaded Ontario.

There the last of the visions came on October 5, 1813. British Capt. William Caldwell, whose father had led the Canadian volunteers at Fallen Timbers, was sitting on a log with Tecumseh awaiting the commencement of the battle of the Thames. The Shawnee, Caldwell remembered, "suddenly started as if shot." When asked if he was all right, he responded that he had seen "an evil spirit that betokens no good." Then, Anthony Shane was told, Tecumseh gave his sword to a friend "to give to his son if he ever grew to be a warrior."

Tecumseh never led the Indians to great victories like those of Little Turtle. But by his conduct as a commander he won a different kind of fame. The Shawnee, Ruddell remembered, "was always averse to taking prisoners in his warfare." But, Tecumseh's friend recalled, he "always expressed the greatest abhorrence when he heard of or saw acts of cruelty or barbarity practiced."

This section of the Constantino Brumidi frieze on the rotunda of the US capitol depicts Tecumseh's death at Thames. (Architect of the Capitol)

When the Shawnee found Indians massacring wounded Kentuckians after Dudley's Defeat on May 5, 1813, he stopped the action. "Who he was I knew not," remembered the wounded Kentuckian George Dale, "but he was the only man that acted like a gentleman, as an officer." Two days later, he found at a nearby Canadian Wyandot camp two of Black Hoof's Shawnees, prisoners who had been badly beaten. Tecumseh ordered them sent back to their villages. By such conduct he won the hearts of enemies he could not defeat in battle.

Tecumseh also failed to become the leader of a united Indian nation. But the grandeur of his vision, and the skill with which he tried to realize it, compelled admiration. "If it were not for the vicinity of the United States," Harrison judged after their second meeting, "he would perhaps be the founder of an empire that would rival in glory Mexico or Peru."

By the time Main Poc died forgotten in 1816, the legend of Tecumseh had captured the imaginations of many Americans. In 1836, when Tenskwatawa died in obscurity, a 16-year-old boy from Lancaster, Ohio, enrolled at West Point with an unusual middle name. While in Harrison's army, William Tecumseh Sherman would write in his memoirs, his father had "caught a fancy for the great chief of the Shawnees, Tecumseh."

But the story of the Prophet and Tecumseh did not end at Thames. One more vision remained to be fulfilled or forgotten. Little Turtle, Black Hoof, and Tarhe had seen at the end of the Shawnee brothers' work civil wars within Indian tribes, the spread of the wars to include the Americans, and an Indian catastrophe. That would occur not on the Northwest Frontier, but far to the south, among the Creeks.

Just before Boyd's regulars departed from Vincennes, Ellipohorchem and his four warriors left Prophetstown to return home. But the Creek was a leader more in the mold of Main Poc than of Tecumseh, and his path led past the Manley cabin near what is now Waverley, Tennessee. There the Creeks found two women and five children, and left with a prisoner and six scalps.

When the horrified Creek chiefs learned of the action, they dispatched three parties of warriors, who tracked and executed the killers. Seekaboo and other Creek shamans then called for revenge. When their followers sent war clubs painted red to all the Creek villages, hundreds of warriors assembled. Known as the Red Sticks, they soon were fighting other Creeks in a tribal civil war.

When it spread to the settlers, it left the American expression "The Good Lord willing and the Creeks don't rise." About 250 joined Creeks loyal to the chiefs in seeking safety at Fort Mims, near present Tensaw, Alabama. On August 13, 1813, Red Stick warriors captured the fort. Of the 517 Americans and Creeks they found there, only 36 escaped.

Andrew Jackson, the commanding general of the Tennessee militia, assembled an army of 2,600 Americans. Pushmataha and William McIntosh recruited 600 Creek, Choctaw, and Cherokee warriors to fight with them. On March 27, 1814, they met the Red Stick army near present Dadeville, Alabama. There, at the battle of Horseshoe Bend, the thing was ended. And when it was over, 757 of the 1,000 Red Stick warriors were dead, and the others were all wounded.

Here, at what is now Horseshoe Bend National Military Park, the fleeing Red Sticks were massacred as they attempted to cross the Tallapoosa River. Their blood briefly turned the Tallapoosa red. (Courtesy of Tennessee History for Kids)

THE BATTLEFIELD TODAY

Museums, parks, and monuments are at the sites of several significant events before and during the campaign that ended at Tippecanoe. The first Prophetstown extended up Mud Creek from what is now Tecumseh Point, a park in Greenville, Ohio. The second Prophetstown was at what is now Prophetstown State Park in Battle Ground, Indiana.

Harrison's mansion in Vincennes, the site of his councils with Tenskwatawa and Tecumseh, is now Grouseland, the William Henry Harrison Mansion and Museum, at 3 W. Scott St. The 1805 territorial capital is a museum at 1 Harrison St. The house of Harrison's spy Michael Brouillet, now the Old French House and Indian Museum, is at 1st and Seminary Sts.

The site of Fort Knox now is a park at 3090 N. Old Fort Knox Road, just north of Vincennes. Fort Harrison was in what is now Terre Haute, Indiana, where a monument in the parking lot of the Landing at Fort Harrison, at 3350 N. 4th St., is at the site. A marker commemorating Harrison's crossing of the Vermilion River is on Ind. Rte. 63, just north of the Vermilion River bridge.

The 6.5-acre battlefield is now Tippecanoe Battlefield Park in Battle Ground, Indiana. The Tippecanoe Battlefield Museum, at 220 Battleground Ave., has extensive exhibits on Harrison's campaign and the battle. Prophet's Rock can be visited on Prophet's Rock Road.

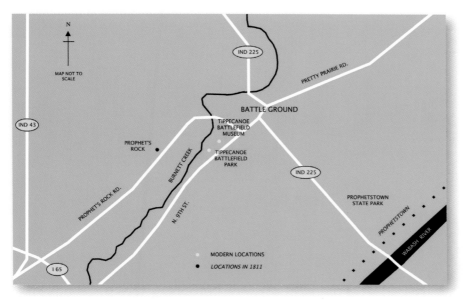

The battlefield today. (Author's map)

FURTHER READING

Anson, Bert, *The Miami Indians* (1970)

Barce, Elmore, "Tecumseh's Confederacy," in *Indiana Magazine of History*, Vol. 12, 161–174 (Indianapolis, 1916); Vol. 13, 67–91 (Indianapolis, 1917)

Beard, Reed, *The Battle of Tippecanoe* (1889)

Byrd, Cecil K., "The Northwest Indians and the British Preceding the War of 1812," in *Indiana Magazine of History*, Vol. 38, 31–50 (Indianapolis, 1924)

Carter, Harvey Lewis, *The Life and Times of Little Turtle: First Sagamore of the Wabash* (1987)

Clark, Jerry E., *The Shawnee* (1977)

Conwell, Rick, *The Battle of Tippecanoe: November 7, 1811* (2013)

Edmunds, R. David, *The Potawatomis* (1978)

Edmunds, R. David, *The Shawnee Prophet* (1983)

Esarey, Logan, ed., *Messages and Letters of William Henry Harrison* (1922)

Larrabee, Charles, "Lieutenant Charles Larrabee's Account of the Battle of Tippecanoe," in *Indiana Magazine of History*, Vol. 57, 225–247 (Indianapolis, 1961)

Lossing, Benson J., *Pictorial Field-Book of the War of 1812* (1868)

McAfee, Robert B., *History of the Late War in the Western Country* (1816)

Naylor, Isaac, "Isaac Naylor's Account of the Battle of Tippecanoe," in *Indiana Magazine of History*, Vol. 4, 163–169 (Indianapolis, 1918)

Owens, Robert M., *Mr. Jefferson's Hammer: William Henry Harrison and the Origins of American Indian Policy* (2007)

Pirtle, Alfred, *The Battle of Tippecanoe* (1900)

Reid, Richard J., *The Battle of Tippecanoe* (1983)

Sugden, John, *Blue Jacket* (2000)

Sugden, John, *Tecumseh* (1997)

Tanner, Helen H., *Atlas of Great Lakes Indian History* (1986)

Tipton, John, "John Tipton's Tippecanoe Journal," in *Indiana Quarterly Magazine of History*, Vol. 2, 179–184 (Indianapolis, 1906)

Tunnell IV, Harry D., *To Compel with Armed Force: A Staff Ride Handbook for the Battle of Tippecanoe* (2000)

Walker, Adam, *A Journal of Two Campaigns of the Fourth Regiment U.S. Infantry in the Indiana and Michigan Territories* (1816)

INDEX

Page numbers in **bold** refer to illustrations and their captions.